This isn't Excel, it's Magic!

Tips and Tricks for getting the most out of Microsoft® Excel

Bob Umlas
Microsoft® Excel MVP

IIL PUBLISHING

IIL Publishing, New York titles may be purchased in bulk at a discount for educational, business, fund-raising, or sales promotional use. For informa- tion, please email michelle.blackley@iil.com or call 212-515-5144.

Microsoft® Excel is a registered trademark of the Microsoft Corporation.

Published by IIL Publishing, New York a division of International Institute for Learning, Inc., 110 East 59th Street, 31st Fl., New York, NY 10022
www.iil.com

ISBN 0-9708276-5-2
Second printing

Edited and designed by Tony Meisel
Publisher Judy Umlas

Printed in the United States of America

I would like to thank my wife, Judy, for her continued support of my pursuing my Excel "studies," which includes time in Redmond for the MVP Summits, as well as my time answering questions in the newsgroups. She also supports my writing this book, given that she's the publisher!

I also want to thank Will Tompkins, my fellow Excel MVPs, my co-workers, and the many other contributors to the online newsgroups – David Hager, John Walkenbach (who has put many of my discoveries of Excel "oddities" on his Web site), Bill Manville, Jim Rech, Jan Karel Pieterse, Tom Chester, Reed Jacobson, Eric Wells, Bob Greenblatt, Tim Aurthur, Monika Weber, Jim Janssen, and Joe Sorrenti for their contributions to my knowledge. Special thanks to Monika Weber for her technical editing of this book.

I want to acknowledge my best friend, Jerry Goldin, Ph.D., for his ongoing support of everything I do and of my entire family. I want to thank my sister, Marilyn Umlas Wachtel, for being there when I have most needed her.

My wonderful children, Stefanie and Jared Umlas, who have put up with my remaining at the computer writing this book, instead of watching *Alias* or *The Simpsons* with them, have been terrific!

I would especially like to thank E. LaVerne Johnson, president and CEO of International Institute for Learning (IIL) for believing that I am one of the top three Excel gurus in the world, no matter what I tell her. I also thank her for supporting my love of teaching by offering the Mastering Microsoft® Excel course through IIL all these years.

– Bob Umlas, Microsoft® Excel MVP

International Institute for Learning, Inc. (IIL)

International Institute for Learning, Inc. (IIL), headquartered in New York City and with eleven operating companies in major cities around the world, is a global leader in Project, Program and Portfolio Management, Microsoft® Project, Six Sigma, and Business Analysis corporate solutions.

Using its Many Methods of Learning™, IIL combines the theory and practice that professionals need in order to manage today's business complexities with maximum flexibility. IIL offers traditional classroom training as well as on-demand learning, "virtual" instructor-led courses, and hands-on leadership simulation classes. IIL recently released *Project Management eLibrary,* a state-of-the art, animated and engaging program that is rich in education and exercises.

Traditional Classroom Learning
Each year IIL schedules hundreds of live, instructor-led courses and workshops in major cities around the world. This offers a convenient and effective way for professionals to participate in classes that expose them to diverse industry perspectives and trainers' real workplace experiences.

Virtual eLearning
Utilizing the latest online technologies, IIL brings professionals a broad curriculum of live, instructor-led courses, including Mastering Microsoft® Excel, via the Internet. This environment allows students to interact live with the instructor and fellow classmates, while avoiding the costs and inconvenience of travel.

On-demand Learning
IIL offers a wide variety of courses that provide extraordinary content along with the convenience of learning at a student's own pace—whether that's at home or work, day or night. In addition to traditional video, texts and workbooks, IIL offers content-rich, multimedia training programs.

Computer-Aided Simulation Learning
A growing number of IIL's courses use computer-aided simulation. This allows participants to learn by making official decisions in a realistic and safe "virtual" business setting.

Onsite Learning and Corporate Solutions
IIL works closely with clients to develop learning solutions that are tailored to meet their precise business objectives and cultural needs.

For more information, please contact:
Lori Milhaven, Executive Vice President
International Institute for Learning, Inc.
Phone: 1–212–515–5121 or 1–800–325–1533
e-mail: Lori.Milhaven@iil.com
www.iil.com

Coming soon from IIL Publishing, New York

The Zen of Project Management
by George Pitagorsky, PMP

The Power of Acknowledgement
by Judith W. Umlas

Project Portfolio Management Tools and Techniques
by Parviz F. Rad, PhD and Ginger Levin, PhD

Project Management Poetry
Original poems submitted to allPM.com
by creative project managers around the globe

Books

Praise for This isn't Excel, it's Magic!

"Bob Umlas is an amazing guy. He has been an Excel MVP since the program began. He has a reputation among the MVPs as being the guy who can find amazing things in Excel. This book contains 85 tips about Excel. I was amazed as I went through the book that I had never heard of at least 50 of these tips! They are cool things that you can do with Excel. Even if you are the Excel guru in your office, you will find new tips in this book. At 150 pages, it is packed with cool stuff."

– Bill Jelen, "Mr. Excel," independent Excel consultant

"I carry *This isn't Excel, It's Magic!* in my car and read tips while stopped at traffic lights. The book is already full of post-it flags for all the tips I didn't know. I think I've flagged all but the title page."

– Melanie Beck, technical training specialist,
Grant County Public Utility District

"I thought I knew a lot about Excel; but I now realize how little I did know. There are so many great head spinning, jaw dropping tips and tricks. It makes unlocking the power of Excel an amazing experience. A must have for (Excel) users everywhere. Mr. Umlas (is) a true magician."

– Alesa Ward, corporate accountant, CM Foods

"I love this book and highly recommend it to all Excel users. Whether you are looking for some simple techniques to make you more productive in Excel, or if you are ready for some sophisticated how-to's, you will learn valuable information from *This isn't Excel, it's Magic!*"

– Bob Schuster, partner of ExcelMagic and
RWS Information Systems

"(*This isn't Excel, it's Magic!* is) a simple, but amazingly useful book. Very clever! Bob has produced a compact, but brilliantly useful book of shortcuts, formula secrets and tricks. One thing I loved about this book is it tackles 'real world' problems. This is not a book for Excel beginners. However, if you use Excel professionally or for fun then you absolutely should consider grabbing a copy of this highly useful and informative book. It will save you many hours of work and delight you at the same time."

– Darryl Collins, Excel/VBA developer

"Nobody willing to use Excel efficiently should be without a copy."
– Miguel Fischman, systems analyst programmer

"What a handy little book chock fill of hints, tips and techniques. I have been studying Excel for longer than I care to admit yet I consider my knowledge of the subject miniscule compared to the author's breadth of skill."
– Chris Curtis, desktop publisher, bellaonline.com

"Bob Umlas is a Microsoft® Most Valuable Professional (MVP) who put his nearly 20 years of Excel experience into a book called: *This isn't Excel, it's Magic!* Bob shares many excellent tips for the experienced Excel user that will save time and energy when working with spreadsheets. A beginner may be a little daunted by some tricks, but will appreciate them once they get to know Excel. The book is well illustrated and narrated."
– Rick Castellini, host of Castellini on Computers

"One of the biggest perks of attending the MVP conference in Redmond was the opportunity to chat with folks from all over the world. I had the unique opportunity to chat with Bob Umlas, an expert in Microsoft® Excel. If you have questions about how to use Microsoft® Excel then Bob probably has the answers."
– David Ciccone, founder, mobilitytoday.com

"The first time I read it was in the middle of the night during a blackout. I had to use a flashlight under the covers. Thanks again for your help."
– Debi Morrison, B2B Support Coordinator,
"the Excel Queen"

"Despite the large selection of accounting software programs for businesses, Microsoft® Excel is the tried-and-true spreadsheet option for most, especially for small businesses. A new book by Bob Umlas, a Microsoft® Excel MVP and author of 300 articles on Excel, shares tips on how to get the most out of the software."
– Accounting Smartpros.com

"You just have to buy this book!"
– Jack Imsdahl, co-host, On Computers
radio show with Alaska Joe

What readers are saying

Contents

Keyboard Shortcuts

Printing

Miscellaneous

Contents

Contents

Microsoft® Excel is probably the most widely-used spreadsheet program in the world. Tens of thousands of businesses and millions of individuals use it for business and personal accounting, projections and plans.

When Excel first shipped in the mid-1980s, I read the manual—yes, Excel came with manuals then—from cover to cover six times, especially in order to learn Data Tables. I have been using it ever since, fascinated by the endless possibilities of the program. Over the years, I have discovered many shortcuts and tricks to make Excel even more efficient and useful.

For example, back in 1993, I attended a seminar given by an ac-knowledged Excel guru. During the session he was hosting for what he called the "Excel SWAT team," he was demonstrating a macro structure using Excel 4-style macros (before VBA existed in Excel), which was quite sophisticated.

He showed a line of code that used a range name—a label—and he wanted to show us the code at that label. So he used Edit/Go to, and we saw hundreds of defined names that he had to laboriously scroll through to get to the one he was looking for. After he had done this about five times, I raised my hand and said, "You know, you can get to that label directly. Just press Ctrl/[." He tried it and was flab-bergasted! So he tried it again. Then he remarked that I just had saved him about two hours every day scrolling through his defined names. When I also told him you could return to the location you were just at by using Ctrl/], he called me the "Excel Trickster," and the nickname has stuck.

My passion for Excel has led me to be a contributing editor to Excellence and The Expert magazines, and I've led sessions at Microsoft's Tech-Ed on tips and tricks and on array formulas. I've also been an Excel MVP for Microsoft since that program's incep-tion—recognition for people who contribute to the online news-groups. Currently, I lead an online Master Class in Excel—12 three-hour sessions (details can be found at http://www.iil.com. Click on "Live eLearning").

All those years of experimentation with Excel have led to this book. I hope you can profit from the tips and tricks, and use them to get the most out of Microsoft® Excel.

– Bob Umlas

1. Using Advanced Filter to another sheet

Advanced filter can only filter to the active sheet.
The active sheet can "pull" information from another sheet, but it cannot "push" information to another sheet. You'd get this message:

But you can pull information to the active sheet:

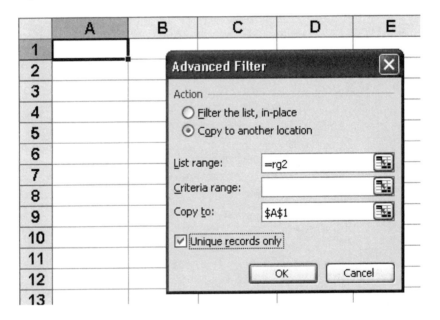

Rg2 is a range defined on another sheet. The sheet we're filtering to is currently empty.

After clicking OK (notice the "Unique" records is checked). You'd see, for example:

	A	B
1	Jared	
2	Fred	
3	Stefanie	
4	Bob	
5	Judy	
6	Alice	
7	Jared	
8	Kate	
9		

2. AutoFormat Toolbar button

You can toggle through all the auto formats by *Shift*-clicking this toolbar button (on a PC, not on a Mac).

The button is found in View/Toolbars/Customize, Command Tab, selecting Format in the Categories listbox, about 7/8 down on the commands listbox:

Click on the Autoformat tool and drag it to a toolbar like the formatting toolbar.

3. *Formatting comments*

When most people create a comment (Insert/Comment, or Shift/F2), they accept the shape and color and just enter the information they want. So most comments look something like this:

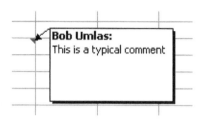

But how about a comment like this:

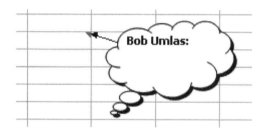

Or even this: (It's me!)

Here's how you can do it.

When you first create a comment, you'll notice that the name box has an indication of what cell the comment is in:

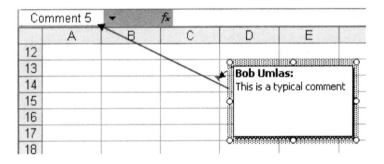

What you need to do is select the *border* of the comment, so you'd see the name of the comment in the name box:

You need the drawing toolbar showing. When the comment is selected this way, select the "Change Autoshape" menu from the Draw toolbar. From that, you can select basic shapes, block arrows, flowchart, stars and banners, or callouts, each of which has yet another set of shapes to choose from. Shown here is the Cloud callout:

Features

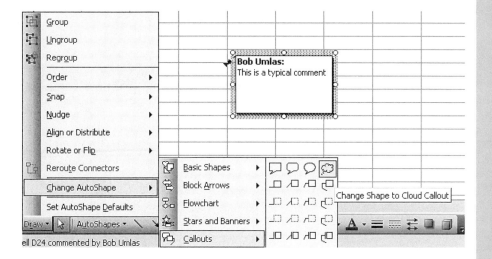

Once you have the new shape, (cloud, here), right-click the border once again and choose Format comment, as shown, if you wish to format this comment even farther:

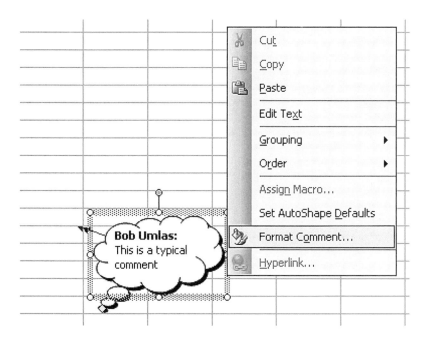

That will bring up yet another dialog, from which you can choose
Fill Effects:

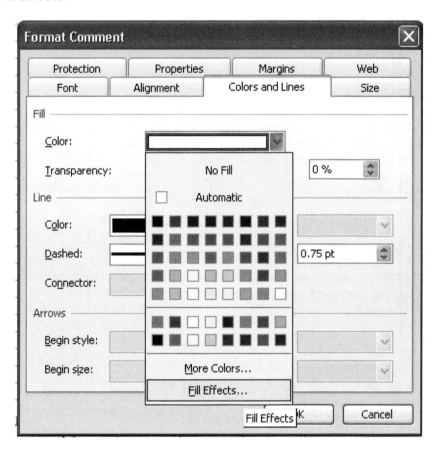

From this dialogue, you can select...

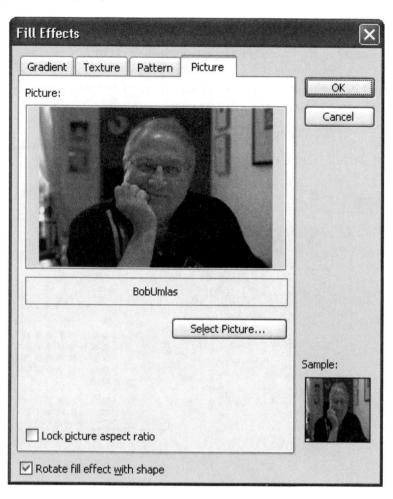

as you saw before.

Features

4. Format #VALUE! or any errors away

Probably the easiest way to not display errors like #VALUE! or #DIV/0! in an already existing worksheet is to use Conditional Formatting. Here's how:

1. Select all the cells you want to hide these error values in.
2. Use Format/Conditional Formatting.
3. Change "Cell Value is" to "Formula Is".
4. Enter =ISERROR(A1) (assuming A1 is the active cell), click the Format button, the font tab, and assign a white font.

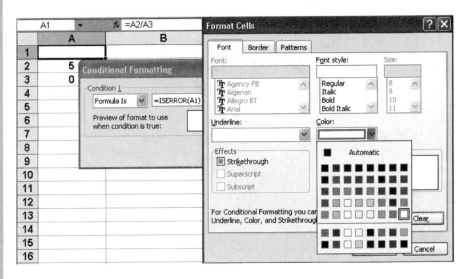

Features

5. Select All 0's;
or Select All specific keyword

Suppose you had a worksheet which looked something like the following, and you wanted to select all the cells *containing* the word "amounts":

	A	B	C
1		Description	
2		m35-c summary input	
3		m35-c gl acount #	
4		m35-c gl description	
5		m35-c amounts	
6		m35-d description	
7		m35-d summary input	
8		m35-d gl acount #	
9		m35-d gl description	
10		m35-d amounts	
11		m80 gl acount #	
12		m80 gl description	
13		m80 ye balance	
14		m80 amounts paid after	
15		m81 gl acount #	
16		m81 gl description	
17		m81 ye balance	
18		m81 amounts paid after	
19		m82 gl acount #	
20		m82 gl description	
21		m82 ye balance	
22		m82 amounts paid after	
23		m83 gl acount #	
24		m83 gl description	
25		m83 ye balance	
26		m83 amounts paid after	
27		m84 gl acount #	
28		m84 gl description	
29		m84 ye balance	
30		m84 amounts paid after	

You can't do it with Edit/Go to Special and use features there, but you can use Excel 2003's Find All, with a twist…

If you use Edit/Find, type in "amounts" (without the quotes), then click the Find All button. You'll see:

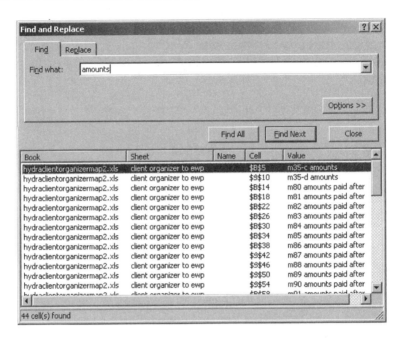

Here's the twist: instead of *selecting* the items in the found list, you can use Ctrl/A (or Shift click the last item in order to select from the already-selected item through the item you're now selecting, or even Ctrl/click to select specific items), and all items selected in the list will also be selected in the worksheet:

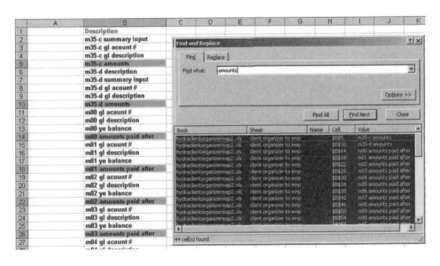

Now, when you close the dialog box, the cells will still be selected.[1]

Now, suppose your worksheet looks something like the following, and you want to change all the italic cells to be bold (and still italic):

	A
1	**Form Name**
2	Form 5471
3	*Form 5471*
4	Form 5471
5	Form 5471
6	*Form 5471*
7	Form 5471
8	Form 5471
9	*Form 5471*
10	Form 5471
11	Form 5471
12	Form 5471
13	Form 5471
14	*Form 5471*
15	*Form 5471*
16	*Form 5471*
17	Form 5471
18	Form 5471
19	*Form 5471*
20	Form 5471
21	Form 5471

---

1 Special thanks to Jan Karel Pieterse for this tip!

Selecting by text now won't do, but there's another feature of Excel 2003's Find command: find by format. Note the Format button at the top:

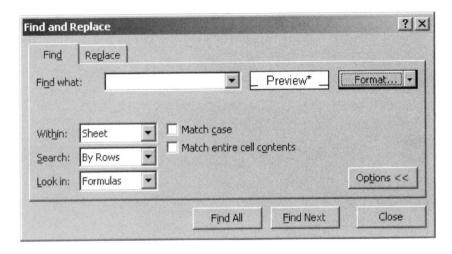

When you click this, you'll see:

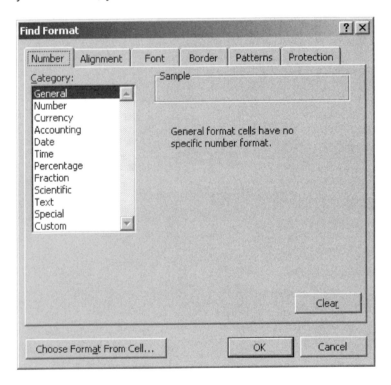

In this dialog, you can enter all the properties of the formatting you're going to want to find, but there's also an easier way: click the bottom button, "Choose Format From Cell..." When you do this, you'll see a special cursor which looks like the regular cell-selection cursor but with an eye-dropper next to it.

When you click on the cell containing the format you want to find, you'll then see a preview of the formatting in the dialog box, and you *can* combine this with text to find as well.

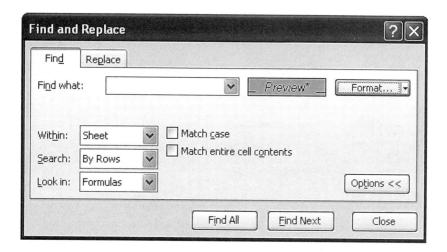

Here's the result:

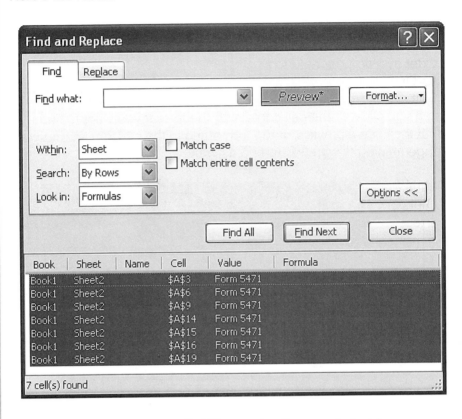

All that's left to do is press Ctrl/B to make those cells bold.

6. Cut/Copy, Insert Paste by dragging borders!

In order for this tip to work, you need to have the setting checked for Tools/Options/Edit/Allow Cell Drag and Drop turned on (which is the default setting anyway).

To cut and paste a range, select it and drag the border (the cursor will change to a cursor with a 4-headed arrow).

To cut and *insert* a range, drag a range by its border *and* the Shift key held down. You will see an indication of where the range will be inserted:

	A	B	C	D
1	36	45	1/1/2003	
2	40	50	2/1/2003	
3	44	55	3/1/2003	
4	48	60	4/1/2003	
5	52	65	5/1/2003	
6	56	70	6/1/2003	A5:C6

The grey line indicates where A1:C2 will be cut and insert-pasted. The intellisense shows that the new location will be at A5:C6.

If you hold the Ctrl key down with either of the two actions above, the cut becomes a copy.

7. Easily create custom list of a-z, A-Z

Instead of typing this all out and then importing to custom lists, you can enter:
=CHAR(ROW()+64) in row 1 and fill down to row 26 for A-Z.

A1	▼	*fx* =CHAR(ROW()+64)		
	A	B	C	D
1	A			
2	B			
3	C			
4	D			
5	E			
6	F			

=CHAR(65) is the letter "A", thru =CHAR(90) is the letter "Z"

The row function returns the row number of the reference.
=ROW(F23) would return 23. If there's no reference, it returns the row that the function is entered in. =ROW() in cell G12 returns 12.

Copy the list and paste special Values (or you won't be able to import them into the Custom Lists).

Then select the range and use Tools/Options/Custom Lists and click Import:

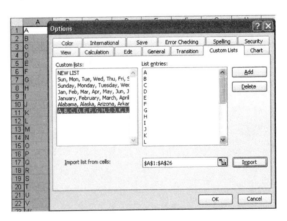

Now, you can enter any letter (upper or lowercase), and use the fill handle. If you entered Uppercase, it will fill with uppercase letters. Lowercase will fill with lowercase letters.

Features

8. Enlarging embedded charts

If your embedded chart has been resized and is too small to work with, moving it to its own sheet makes it easy to work with, but returning it to its original sheet loses its original size.

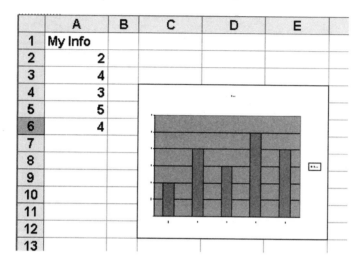

Right-click the chart, select Chart Window...

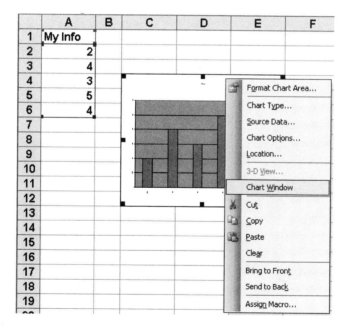

That puts the chart into its own window:

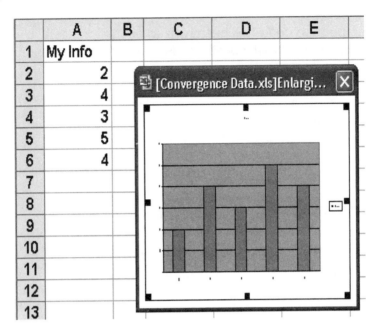

Resize this to work with by dragging the corners of the border. When you close it, the original chart size is left intact.

Features

9. Use Fill-handle to insert or delete rows

Did you know that holding the Shift down while using the fill handle will *Shift* cells? Well, now you do. Let's take a look.

1. Hold Shift key while dragging Fill Handle. You will see a new shape to the fill handle, a split vertical 2-headed arrow.
2. If drag down, you will insert rows
3. If drag up, you will delete rows
4. If drag right, you will insert columns
5. If drag left, you will delete columns

10. Shift/find finds backwards

This is great for finding the last department in a list, for example:

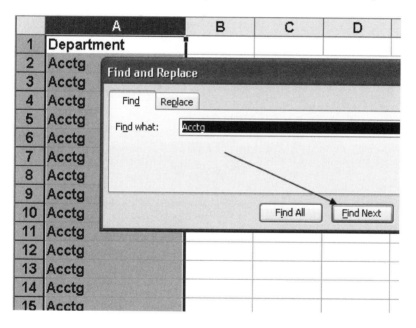

Features

How can you tell where the last Acctg department is? Use Edit/Find, and before clicking Find Next, hold the Shift key, and you're there in one click.

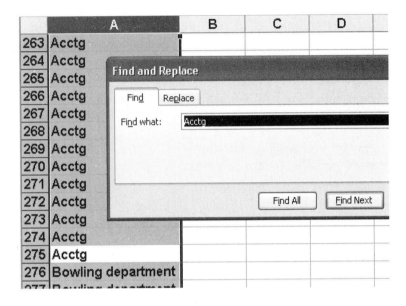

You can use a wildcard to search for *anything* backwards, so starting from cell A1, you can find the last row or column.

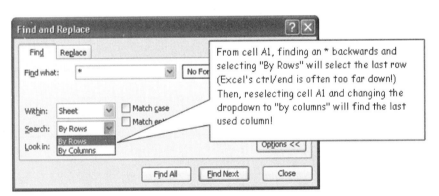

From cell A1, finding an * backwards and selecting "By Rows" will select the last row (Excel's ctrl/end is often too far down!) Then, reselecting cell A1 and changing the dropdown to "by columns" will find the last used column!

11. Using [h] format for hours>=24

When you add times, anything over 23:59:59 will start over at 0. If you use a format of [h]:mm:ss then you will get the "true" number of hours:

	C6	▼	*fx* =SUM(B1:B5)	
	A	**B**	**C**	
1		3:15		
2		4:15		
3		5:15		
4		6:15		
5		7:15		
6	Total Time	2:15	26:15	

The formulas in B6 and C6 are identical. However, B6 is formatted as h:mm:ss which will not permit the "h" to be above 23, and the format for cell C6 is [h]:mm:ss.

12. Advanced number formatting

You can specify formatting by value ranges. This format:
[Red][<80]"TOO LOW";[Blue][>120]"TOO HIGH";$#,##0.00
says: if the value in the cell is <80, make it red and show the text "TOO LOW". If the value in the cell is >120, make it blue and display the text "TOO HIGH". Otherwise, format it as currency.

Aside from [red], [blue], [cyan], [magenta], [white], [black], [blue], and [green], you can use [color1] thru [color56].

The rule is to place the color inside square brackets, followed by another set of square brackets for the condition, then the format if it meets that condition. You're limited to 2 conditions plus an "all other".

Features

13. Formatting text

You can have parts of text constants in one cell be different sizes, fonts, color, by selecting the text and using the tools from the formatting toolbar. (This will not work for formulas.)

Text can be formatted by characters in a cell (*not* formulas)

Here:

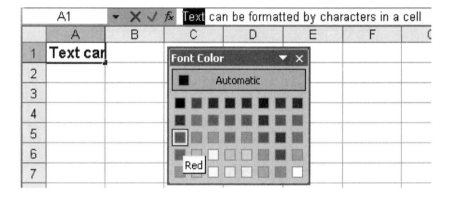

The word "Text" is selected in the formula bar, and the red font color is being applied. Only the word "Text" will be red.

14. Inner Series

Some functions take a parameter which changes, like
=IPMT(rate,per,nper,pv,fv,type)

The "per" argument usually differs from one row to the next, making it difficult to fill down. Most people enter the series 1;2;3;... down a column for the sole purpose of being able to reference it in the formula. Instead, use ROW(A1) as the "per" argument:

	A	B	C	D	E
	B6 ▾	*fx* =IPMT($B$1/12,ROW(A1),$B$2*12,-$B$3)			
1	Rate	5.25%			
2	Nper	30			
3	PV	$ 400,000			
4					
5					
6		$1,750.00			
7		$1,747.99			
8		$1,745.98			
9		$1,743.95			
10		$1,741.92			
11		$1,739.88			
12		$1,737.82			
13		$1,735.76			

When the formula in cell B6 is filled down, the part containing ROW(A1) becomes ROW(A2), etc. This is, of course, 1 in B6, 2 in B7, etc, giving the inner series.

You can also use column(A1), of course, if the series needs to be filled right.

Features

15. Using Insert/Name/Apply

Immediately after naming ranges, you can easily apply these names to existing references. For example, if you have =B5+B6 in a cell

| B2 | ▼ | ƒ× | =B5+B6 |

	A	B	C
1			
2		11	
3			
4			
5	First	4	
6	Second	7	

and then name B5 "First" and B6 "Second" (by using Insert/Name/Create),

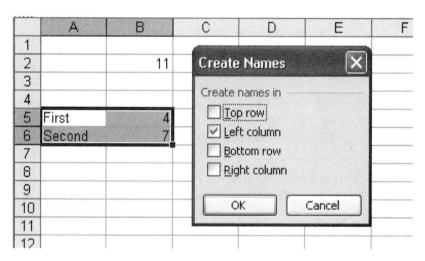

then after naming them you can use Insert/Name/Apply, and these will already be selected in the dialog:

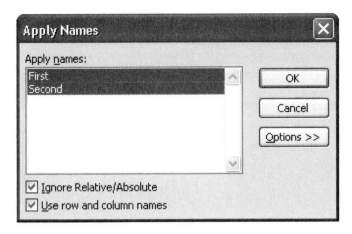

After you apply the names you will see =First+Second

16. Combining cells with Paste Special/Skip blanks

You've *seen* the Skip Blanks feature in the Paste Special dialog, but do you know how to use it? It refers to the range being copied— blank cells in the *source* won't erase cells in the *receiving* range.

Example:
A1:A7 has a,,c,,e,,g and B1:B7 has b,,d,,f,,h:

Copy B1:B7, select A2, Paste Special with Skip blanks:

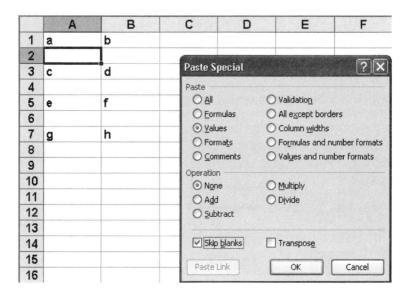

Here's the result:

17. Selecting random sample of data

If you have a database with many records and you want to take a random sample of that data, here are a few techniques you can use.

One way to get a random sample is to use a computed criteria and advanced filter.

Suppose you want to take a random 10% of the data. Enter the formula as shown in C2 (keep C1 blank). By entering the formula =RAND()<0.1, every time this worksheet calculates, the =RAND() will return another random number. So RAND()<0.1 will return TRUE, about 10% of the time.

(Rand() returns a random value between 0 and 1, not including 1.)

C2	▼	f_x =RAND()<0.1	
	A	B	C
1	Database of 100 items		
2	Item1		TRUE
3	Item2		
4	Item3		
5	Item4		
6	Item5		
7	Item6		
8	Item7		
9	Item8		
10	Item9		

Features

Using Data/Filter/Advanced filter like this:

will create a random selection:

	A
1	Database of 100 items
27	Item26
38	Item37
49	Item48
59	Item58
71	Item70
78	Item77
87	Item86
92	Item91
99	Item98
102	

This will be different each time. You may notice that there are only 9 items shown, not 10, and that's because the values RAND returns are random. It's best to use this on larger databases.

A second way to select a random 10% of your data is to still use the RAND function but not use filtering. Look at this:

	B2	▾	*f*x =RAND()	
	A		**B**	
1	**Database of 100 items**			
2	Item1		0.07321	
3	Item2		0.912299	
4	Item3		0.331593	
5	Item4		0.743234	
6	Item5		0.511872	
7	Item6		0.577745	
8	Item7		0.863263	
9	Item8		0.155742	
10	Item9		0.827113	
11	Item10		0.585801	

Cells B2 thru B101 contain =RAND(). All you need do is select A2:B101 and sort by column B! Take just the first 10 items, and you have your random 10% of the database.

18. Right-click drag the Fill Handle for several options

If you use the fill handle and drag with the right-mouse down, you will be presented with a dialog containing several options when you let go of the mouse button:

	A	B	C	D	E
1	36	45	1/1/2003		
2	40	50	2/1/2003		
3				3/1/2003	
4				Copy Cells	
5				Fill Series	
6				Fill Formatting Only	
7					
8				Fill Without Formatting	
9				Fill Days	
10				Fill Weekdays	
11				Fill Months	
12				Fill Years	
13				Linear Trend	
14				Growth Trend	
15				Series...	
16					

What the original selection contains will determine what options are available in the dialog:

	A	B	C
1	36	45	1/1/2003
2	40	50	2/1/2003
3			
4		Copy Cells	
5		Fill Series	
6		Fill Formatting Only	
7		Fill Without Formatting	
8		Fill Days	
9		Fill Weekdays	
10			
11		Fill Months	
12		Fill Years	
13		Linear Trend	
14		Growth Trend	
15		Series...	

Notice that in the first example, dates were selected, so the middle section of the dialog (filling dates) is available, but the second example has the middle section disabled because dates weren't selected. The Fill Weekdays option with dates selected can be quite useful:

	A	B	C
1	36	45	1/6/2005
2	40	50	1/7/2005
3			1/10/2005
4			1/11/2005
5			1/12/2005
6			1/13/2005
7			1/14/2005
8			1/17/2005
9			1/18/2005

Cell C1's fill handle was dragged down to cell C9 with the right mouse used, and Fill Weekdays was chosen. Notice 1/8, 1/9, 1/15, and 1/16 are missing, because they're weekends.

Features

19. How to change row height when a key field changes

Suppose you had a worksheet something like this (but more complicated!)

	A	
1	Department	
2	Accounting	
3	Accounting	
4	Accounting	
5	Accounting	
6	Accounting	
7	Accounting	
8	Accounting	
9	Accounting	
10	Personnel	
11	Personnel	
12	Personnel	
13	Personnel	
14	Personnel	
15	IS	
16	IS	
17	IS	

If A1:A3000 contains departments (sorted) and you want a visual break between departments you can change row heights on the first row of each new one. How can you select the changed department? In the above example, in cell B2, e.g., enter a formula such as =IF(A1=A2,1,NA()).

Or you could enter =IF(A1=A2,TRUE,"X").

The choices I'm using are *any* two of Number, Text, Logical, Error because of this:

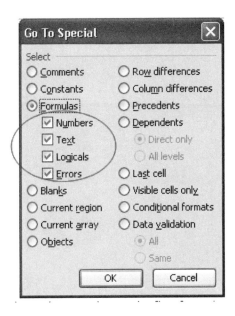

Assuming we choose the first formula, then the NA()'s will show on every new department:

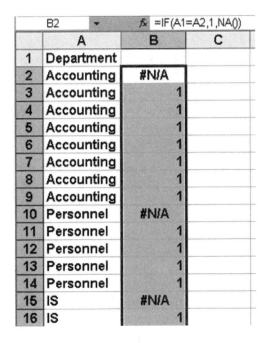

	B2 ▼	f_x =IF(A1=A2,1,NA())	
	A	**B**	**C**
1	Department		
2	Accounting	#N/A	
3	Accounting	1	
4	Accounting	1	
5	Accounting	1	
6	Accounting	1	
7	Accounting	1	
8	Accounting	1	
9	Accounting	1	
10	Personnel	#N/A	
11	Personnel	1	
12	Personnel	1	
13	Personnel	1	
14	Personnel	1	
15	IS	#N/A	
16	IS	1	

Features

Select B:B, Edit/Go to Special, select Formulas + Errors (you actually have to *deselect* Numbers, Text, and Logicals, leaving just Errors, or just deselect Numbers because you know the result is only numbers and errors):

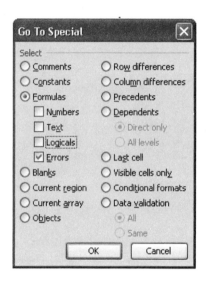

Now only the #N/A cells are selected, so you can use Format/Row/Height/30:

	A	B
1	Department	
2	Accounting	#N/A
3	Accounting	1
4	Accounting	1
5	Accounting	1
6	Accounting	1
7	Accounting	1
8	Accounting	1
9	Accounting	1
10	Personnel	#N/A
11	Personnel	1
12	Personnel	1
13	Personnel	1
14	Personnel	1
15	IS	#N/A
16	IS	1

And finally you can clear column B.

20. Sorting columns

This is useful for rearranging columns and is often easier that cut/insert paste to move the columns around.

You may have to use a "dummy" row to enter the sort sequence. In this worksheet, a dummy row was inserted (row 1) to enter the sort sequence. We want Name, then Address, then city, state, and zip.

	A	B	C	D	E
1	2	1	4	3	5
2	Address	Name	State	City	Zip
3	123 Main	Name1	FL	Orlando	12345
4	124 Main	Name2	NY	Albany	12346
5	125 Main	Name3	WA	Redmond	12347
6	126 Main	Name4	TX	Houston	12348
7	127 Main	Name5	CA	Orlando	12349
8	128 Main	Name6	FL	Albany	12350

Use Data/Sort, Click the "Options" button, click Sort Left-to-Right,

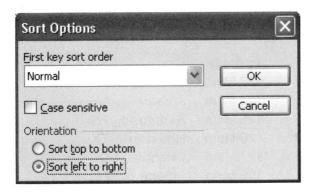

Features

click OK,

then pick the row containing the desired column sequence, and click OK:

	A	B	C	D	E
1	1	2	3	4	5
2	Name	Address	City	State	Zip
3	Name1	123 Main	Orlando	FL	12345
4	Name2	124 Main	Albany	NY	12346
5	Name3	125 Main	Redmond	WA	12347
6	Name4	126 Main	Houston	TX	12348
7	Name5	127 Main	Orlando	CA	12349
8	Name6	128 Main	Albany	FL	12350
9	Name7	129 Main	Redmond	NY	12351

21. Tear-off palettes

There are many toolbar buttons which can be made to float, so you have quicker access to their contents. Some of these are Font, Fill, Borders, Draw…

To make them floating, follow these steps:
1. Click on the arrow next to the button (they all have them) to make the contents drop down.
2. Slowly move the cursor down to the tool's "border" until it gets highlighted and you see the tip (in this example, it says "Drag to make this menu float"):

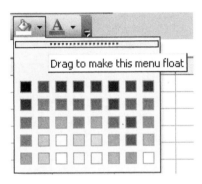

3. Drag the menu by this border into the workbook environment:

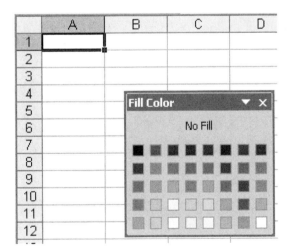

4. From the drawing toolbar, you can access the flowcharting drawing objects to make them float as well:

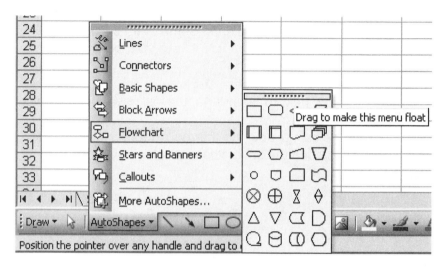

5. The AutoShapes toolbar has an interesting property, since all of its menus are submenus. If you make it float:

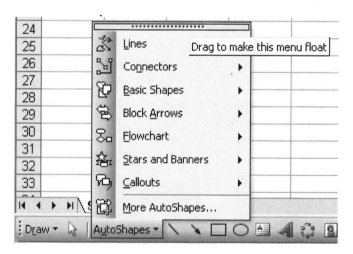

then it looks like this:

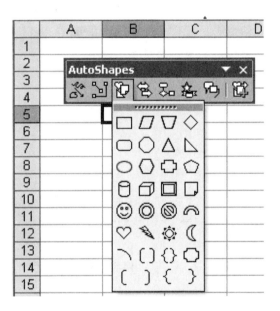

And each of these is a tear-off palette:

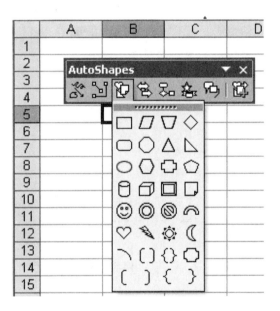

Features

6. Here's a picture of many of the floating palettes:

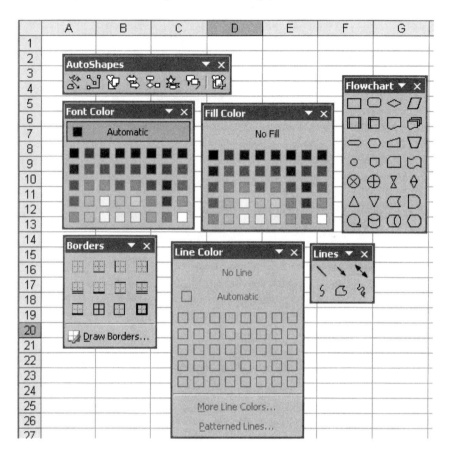

You close them with the "x" in the upper right corner.

22. Define "global/local" name

If you define a name to reference the cell above by using Insert/ Name, like from D2 you define "above" to be =D1, Excel puts the sheet name in front of it:

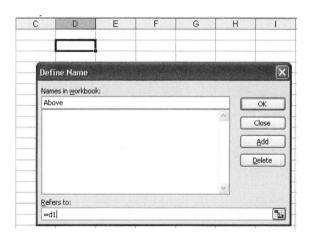

Assuming the active sheet is is Sheet 2, you get "above" to be =Sheet2!D1:

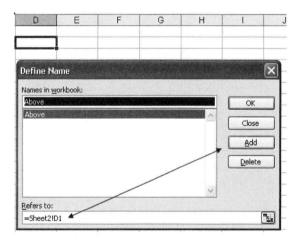

So any time I use =Above to reference the cell above the active cell, it will *always* pick the cell from Sheet2. That is, if on Sheet2 cell A1 I have "Bob," then if I enter =Above from Sheet1 cell A2, I'd see "Bob."

Interesting side note: if the active cell is in row 1 and you use Edit/Go To and type Above, the active cell will be in row 65536!.

To get "above" to be the cell above on *any* sheet, do one of the following:

1. Leave leading "!"... that is, define "above" to be =!D1:

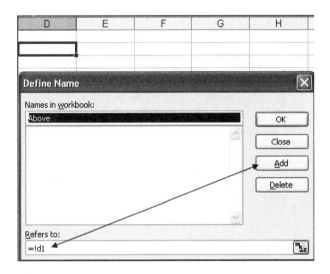

2. Define "above" to be =INDIRECT("r[-1]c",FALSE)

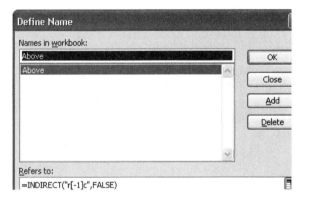

The difference between the 2 choices is that the latter will calculate automatically, and the former won't (without *forcing* a calculation with the F9 key).

As a side note, you probably shouldn't use this technique if you're also using VBA because there's a bug that when VBA recalculates, all cells with that name refer to the active worksheet.

23. XLM-names (not XML)

Old style Excel 4 macros ("XLM"=eXceL Macros) are still around and useful.

They *must* be used as a defined name, not as a worksheet function. If you try to use these as worksheet functions, Excel will give you an error. (Please note that prior to version 2003, copying a cell which uses this name to another sheet will crash Excel.)

For example, the LINKS function will return a list of the links in the workbook (and in a way that you can see the entire path!)
=LINKS()

This will return all the file names in the current directory.
=FILES()

This will return the names in the workbook.
=NAMES()

There are *many* more, and if you're interested, you can download them from *http://support.microsoft.com/kb/q128185/*

Example: Define lk as =LINKS(). Then use =INDEX(lk,1) to get first link, or =INDEX(lk,row()) in row 1 & fill down to get all the links:

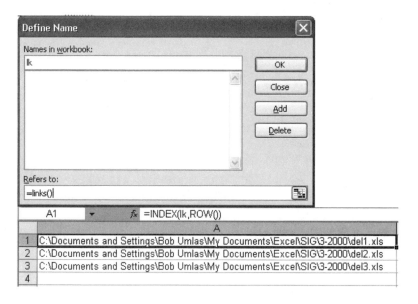

As you can see, cell A1 contains the formula as indicated, and it returns the entire link path to the first link document. The workbook is linked to 3 workbooks, named del1.xls, del2.xls, and del3.xls. But the Edit/Links dialog doesn't show the whole path:

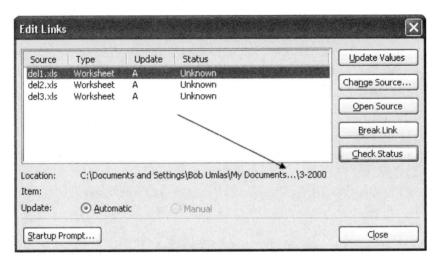

Similarly, here's the file/open dialog:

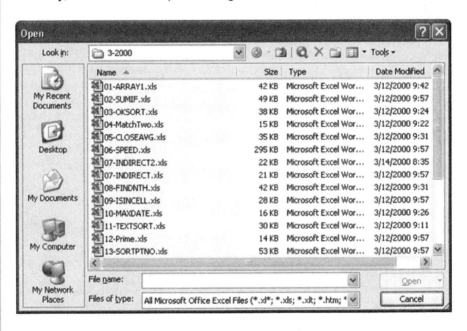

By defining a name like FL, for example, to be =FILES(), you can get this directly into your worksheet:

A1	▼	f_x =INDEX(FL,ROW())

	A	B	C
1	01-ARRAY1.xls		
2	02-SUMIF.xls		
3	03-OKSORT.xls		
4	04-MatchTwo.xls		
5	05-CLOSEAVG.xls		
6	06-SPEED.xls		
7	07-INDIRECT.xls		
8	07-INDIRECT2.xls		
9	08-FINDNTH.xls		
10	09-ISINCELL.xls		
11	10-MAXDATE.xls		
12	11-TEXTSORT.xls		
13	12-Prime.xls		
14	13-SORTPTNO.xls		
15	14-WILCOX.xls		
16	15-UNQINSEQ.xls		
17	16-CALENDAR.xls		

Another nice feature of this is that you can filter on the files. For example, if you wanted to return only those files which have an "O" in them, you can use =FILES("*O*") where the asterisks are wildcards:

24. Defining names for large non-contiguous ranges

If you need to name a multi-area range, you're limited to about 255 characters in the definition. This can cause problems as seen here. In this worksheet we want to give a name to all the cells containing values so that it's easy to clear them or add them up, or refer to them in some way.

	A	B	C	D	E	F	G	H	I
1	Data:	2							
2				Data:	22				
3	Data:	25				Data:	21	Data:	27
4				Data:	24				
5						Data:	63		
6	Data:	12		Data:	25				
7	Data:	14							
8						Data:	89		
9						Data:	63	Data:	81
10				Data:	50	Data:	70		
11	Data:	33							
12				Data:	88				
13									
14	Data:	30				Data:	105		
15									

This tab has a long name / Sheet2 / Sheet3 /

Also notice the tab's name is quite long.

We want to name the cells, so we select them first (it's easiest using Edit/Go to Special) and making this selection:

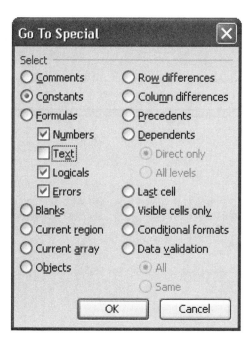

That is, we're selecting constants which are numbers (not text). Then we use Insert/Name/Define:

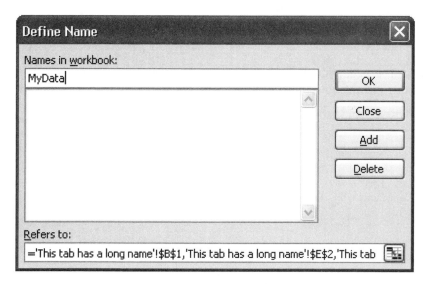

Notice the long tab name is part of the definition. This part has a limit, so we might get a message such as:

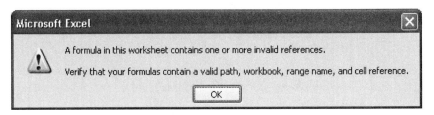

And upon clicking OK, see

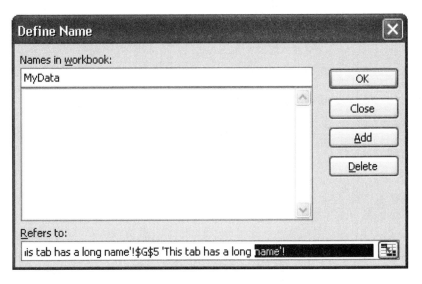

The name is too long! And also notice that the last reference in the Refers to in the above dialog box is to cell G5. Our cells that need naming go down to G14. Well, this is not going to work.

Since the definition includes the tab name, you can temporarily change the name to a single character to get more cells defined:

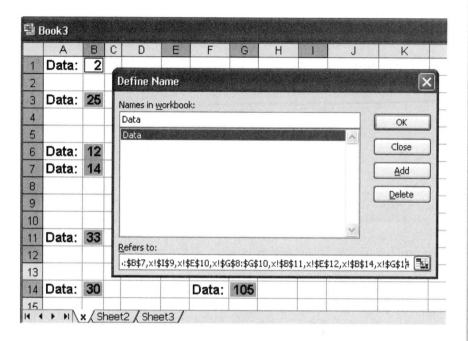

Changing the name of the tab to "x", enables all the cells to be referenced. (I scrolled the information in the Refers to box to the right so you can see that it does end in G14.)

By changing the tab name back to the original, it still maintains all the references.

Another way you can accomplish this is to give names to the cells in pieces, like part1, part2, part3, where part1 may refer to the first 5 cells, part 2 the 2nd 5, etc., and have the "real" name be a reference to the union of all the parts:
Define "all" as =part1,part2,part3

Features

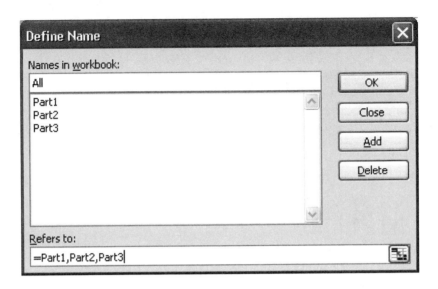

Then any reference to All will reference all the cells.

Perhaps the best way of all, in most cases, is to name the cells by simply typing the name in the name box:

	A	B	C	D	E	F	G
1	Data:	2					
2				Data:	22		
3	Data:	25				Data:	21
4							
5						Data:	63
6	Data:	12		Data:	25		
7	Data:	14					
8						Data:	89
9						Data:	63
10				Data:	50	Data:	70
11	Data:	33					

(Name box: MyInfo, fx 2)

which seems to work even with a long tab name. This last technique fails on VERY many cells, around 224 of them, but you can then revert to the tip above to name them in sections and combine them as shown in the definition of "All".

You can actually name thousands of non-contiguous ranges at once! Select them all, switch to VBA (Alt/F11), use the immediate pane (ctrl/ G), then enter: Selection.Name="TheRangeNameGoesHere"!!

25. What is that :1, :2... I see in the workbook title?

Window/New Window creates another "view" of the same workbook.

You can use it to:
View separate sheets of the same workbook at the same time:

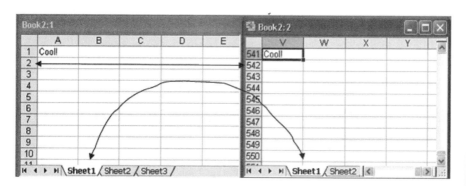

View the same sheet but remote areas simultaneously:

View formulas and values simultaneously:

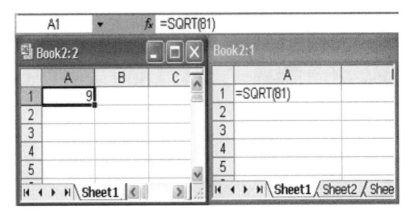

To rejoin the windows, close the window by the "x" in the upper right, not by File/Close, because the separate windows would save and reopen that way. You can do Window/New Window many times and get as many windows as you wish of the workbook.

Think of it as if you were looking out your physical window and seeing parked cars. Now move to another window and look at the same cars. You have a slightly different perspective of the same object. That's kind of what's going on here.

If you use Tools/Options/View tab, you will see many options at the bottom specifically for Windows, not workbooks or worksheets.

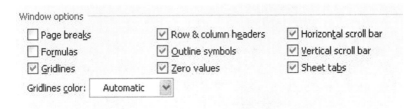

Any of these settings can be seen simultaneously with other windows' settings!

26. One toolbar button, 2 uses

Holding the Shift key down when you click some toolbar buttons and some menus items changes them.

Shift/click the Open toolbar button becomes Save;
Shift/click the Print toolbar button becomes Print Preview;
    …Sort ascending becomes descending;
    …align left becomes right;
    …increase decimal becomes decrease decimal;
Underline becomes double underline.

With menus, File/Close becomes File/Close All; Edit/Copy becomes Edit/Copy picture, and so on.

Experiment with them. If you find your buttons are getting crowded, you can eliminate some of them knowing that they're there but "hidden" under the Shift key press.

27. Double-clicking tools

Double-click the format painter keeps it "alive" to click on several cells without having to click the tool again.

Double-click a drawing tool (rectangle, for example) to draw several without revisiting the tool.

Press the esc key to stop that feature or click the tool again.

Features

28. Getting number of unique values

For this example, assume Rg is defined as A1:A10 and contains
4;5;5;4;5;5;4;5;5;5

    Array-enter[2*] =SUM(1/COUNTIF(Rg,Rg))
    (Ctrl+Shift+Enter)

How it works:
First, a brief discussion of the COUNTIF formula. The syntax is
=COUNTIF(Range,Criteria). It counts the number of items in the range
which meet the criteria. So, in our example, =COUNTIF(Rg,4) would
return 3, because there are 3 4's in the range. Similarly,
=COUNTIF(Rg,5) would return 7 because there are 7 5's.

It turns out that if you use the range itself as the criteria, then each
item in the range is used, one at a time, as the criteria.

So, COUNTIF(Rg,Rg) counts the number if 4's, then counts the # of
5's, then counts the # of 5's, etc. This returns ={3;7;7;3;7;7;3;7;7;7}.
However, you will only *see* the first value, 3, in the cell. If you clicked
in the formula bar and pressed the F9 key (calculate), you'd see all
the values. (If you did this, don't forget to either press esc to cancel
the calculation or click the X near the formula bar.)

So now, 1/COUNTIF(Rg,Rg) returns ={1/3,1/7,1/7,1/3,1/7,1/7,1/3,1/7,
1/7,1/7}.
There are 3 "1/3", and 7 "1/7", each totaling 1.
So the SUM returns the correct result: There are 2 unique values.

This needs to be Ctrl/Shift/entered or it will calculate as if that first 3
were the only value, and the answer would be 1/3, or .333333333.

---

2 For a complete understanding of Array-formulas, visit my website at http://www.
emailoffice.com/excel/arrays-bobumlas.html

29. Named formulas are array-entered

If the formula in the preceding tip were entered without Ctrl+Shift, the cell would contain .33333, as mentioned.

If a name (say "unique") is defined to be =SUM(1/COUNTIF(Rg,Rg)) and you enter =unique, without pressing Ctrl+Shift, the cell would contain 2.

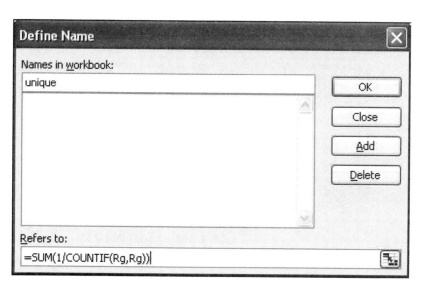

So it seems *all* named formulas are treated the same as if you entered it as an array-formula.

However, here's an oddity. If you enter =A1:A2 in cell A3, you'd see #VALUE!. If you array-enter it, you see whatever is in cell A1. If, while the cursor is in cell A3, you define a name to be =A1:A2, then entering that name in A3 still produces #VALUE! If you array-enter that name (like {=test}—the braces supplied by Excel) then it returns A1's value. So these techniques seem to contradict one another.

Just be aware that your named formulas *may* be different from what you expect only because it's likely interpreted as array-entered.

Formulas

30. Auto-number questions

If you have a numbered questionnaire, it can be cumbersome to move items around or delete because the numbering of the questions has to be redone. Instead, use a formula in A2 such as =MAX(A$1:A1)+1. This means the largest number from cell A1 to the cell above, plus 1. In cell A11, this formula reads =MAX(A$1:A10)+1.

Now, inserting or deleting renumbers all questions!

	A11	▼	f_x	=MAX(A$1:A10)+1
	A	**B**	**C**	
1	Question#	Question		
2	1	Blah blah blah blah bl		
3		Blah blah blah blah bl		
4		Blah blah blah blah bl		
5		Blah blah blah blah bl		
6				
7	2	Blah blah blah blah bl		
8		Blah blah blah blah bl		
9		Blah blah blah blah bl		
10				
11	3	Blah blah blah blah bl		
12		Blah blah blah blah bl		
13		Blah blah blah blah bl		
14				
15	4	Blah blah blah blah bl		
16		Blah blah blah blah bl		

You can see that the largest # in A1:A10 is 2. 2+1 is 3, so A11 contains 3. If I decided to remove question 3, I could delete rows 10:13 (or 11:14) and the 4 which is now in A15 would become 3! As a matter of fact, if I inserted 5 rows at row 10 and inserted a NEW question, as long as I numbered it with the same formula, all the numbers below would also renumber.

31. AutoSum Tool features

Suppose you have a block of cells like in this illustration, containing numbers which you want to enter the totals both on the right and below; that is, in E1:E7 and A8:E8. You'd probably do it something like this:

	A	B	C	D	E	F
1	65	54	30	46	=SUM(A1:D1)	
2	84	85	87	74	SUM(number1, [num	
3	14	69	78	97		
4	88	42	71	6		
5	5	32	71	62		
6	57	47	65	2		
7	50	5	63	92		
8						

1. Click in E1 and click the Sum tool and press enter (or double-click the Sum tool).
2. Click the fill handle in E1 and drag to E7, or double click the fill handle in E1.
3. Select cell A8, click the sum tool, enter the formula, select the fill handle, drag to E8.

Hold on to your hats. It can all be done in one click:
Make this selection as shown in the illustration (A1:E8):

	A	B	C	D	E
1	65	54	30	46	
2	84	85	87	74	
3	14	69	78	97	
4	88	42	71	6	
5	5	32	71	62	
6	57	47	65	2	
7	50	5	63	92	
8					

Select an extra blank column and row.
Click AutoSum Tool once, and you're done!

Formulas

Next, if you have a multi-cell selection, as in this illustration:

	A	B
1	60	60
2	54	66
3	58	28
4	57	16
5	9	14
6		91
7	34	29
8	70	16
9	62	
10	70	7
11	66	68
12	95	77
13	76	13
14	46	84
15	32	70
16		18
17		

A *single* click of the sum tool will put the correct totals in:

	A	B
1	60	60
2	54	66
3	58	28
4	57	16
5	9	14
6	238	91
7	34	29
8	70	16
9	62	320
10	70	7
11	66	68
12	95	77
13	76	13
14	46	84
15	32	70
16	551	18
17		337

32. *Getting end of month*

You don't need the Analysis Toolpak (an add-in which ships with Excel). If the date is in cell A1, then to get the date of the last day of that month, use =DATE(YEAR(A1),MONTH(A1)+1,0).

The DATE function takes 3 parameters: year, month, and day. The Year is the same year as cell A1's year, so we simply use YEAR(A1). MONTH(A1)+1 is one month past the month in cell A1.

The *first* day of *next* month is =DATE(YEAR(A1),MONTH(A1)+1,1), so the day *before* that is last day of *this* month. Therefore, instead of using 1 as the day parameter, Excel has no problem with using 0.

The Month parameter for the DATE function doesn't need to be 1-12, and the Day parameter doesn't need to be 1-31.

Of course, you can also use =DATE(YEAR(A1),MONTH(A1)+1,1)-1 if you don't like using 0 for the day parameter.

Formulas

33. Change dates like 20050923 to one Excel can "understand"

Suppose you are looking at a worksheet which contains dates which can't be formatted as "real" dates because of their structure:

	A	B
1	20050923	
2	20050930	
3	20051107	
4		
5		
6		

Select the date(s), and use Data/Text-To-Columns, which brings up the Text-to-Columns wizard:

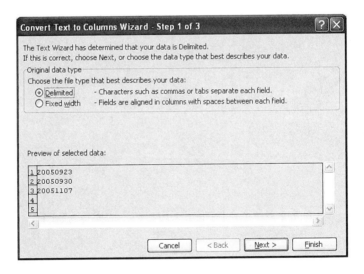

Even though the dates are fixed width, in this case you can simply click "Next" twice.

In step 3 of wizard Select Date, YMD:

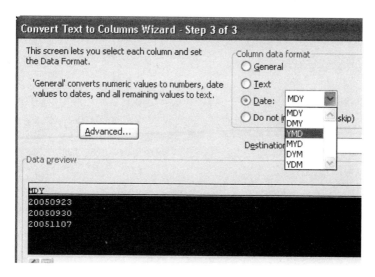

If you click Finish now, the result will replace the dates. You can select another destination cell:

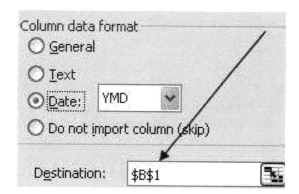

Here's the result:

	A	B	C
1	20050923	9/23/2005	
2	20050930	9/30/2005	
3	20051107	11/7/2005	
4			

34. How many Wednesdays between 1/1/05 and now?

Not limited to Wednesdays!

Use the INDIRECT function to turn the date into a range!! (Hang in there!)

If A1 has 1/1/05 and A2 has =TODAY() (and let's assume for this example that today is 3/5/05)
=ROW(INDIRECT(A1&":"&A2)) is the same as
=ROW(INDIRECT("38353:38416")) which is the same as
{38353;38354...38415;38416}.

You can see this effect by dragging the cursor across A1&":&A2 in the formula and pressing the F9-key. Be sure to press the esc key after pressing the F9-key so that the expansion of the formula will not be permanent.

These numbers are "serial" numbers, Excel's way of numbering days since 1/1/1900.

The INDIRECT function changes text to a range, where possible.

The WEEKDAY function takes a date and returns the day of the week, where 1=Sunday, 2=Monday, etc. So, =WEEKDAY(ROW(INDIRECT(A1&":"&A2))) would return {7;1;2;3...} because 1/1/05 is a Saturday, and Saturday is 7, so it starts with 7.

Put another way, =WEEKDAY(38353), where 38353 is the serial # for 1/1/05, is 7.

Comparing this sequence of numbers—{7;1;2;3} - to a 4 changes these numbers to a series of True/False values:

A3	▼	*fx* {=WEEKDAY(ROW(INDIRECT(A1&":"&A2)))=4}			
	A	**B**	**C**	**D**	**E**
1	1/1/2005				
2	3/5/2005				
3	**FALSE**				

—expanding the formula bar (clicking anywhere in the formula bar and pressing the F9-key) shows:

OFFSET	▼ ✕ ✓ fx	={FALSE;FALSE;FALSE;FALSE;TRUE;FALSE;FALSE;FALSE;FALSE;FALS
	A	B	TRUE;FALSE;FALSE;FALSE;FALSE;FALSE;FALSE;TRUE;FALSE;FALSE;F
1	1/1/2005		FALSE;FALSE;FALSE;TRUE;FALSE;FALSE;FALSE;FALSE;FALSE;FALSE
2	3/5/2005		FALSE;FALSE;FALSE;FALSE;FALSE;FALSE;TRUE;FALSE;FALSE;FALSE
3	FALSE}		

...the TRUE values correspond to Wednesdays.
The N function changes False to 0, True to 1:
Then the Sum Function adds them all up.

Array-entering =SUM(N(WEEKDAY(ROW(INDIRECT(A1&":"&A2)))=4)) gives 9, meaning there are 9 Wednesdays between 1/1/05 and 3/5/05.

35. Looking up 2 (or more) values

Suppose you have a table of values looking something like this:

	A	B	C	D	E	F	G
1	Master List						Find
2	First	Last	Amount			Bob	Williams
3	Bob	Smith	23			Fred	Williams
4	Fred	Williams	78			Bob	Clinton
5	Bob	Devon	45				
6	Bob	Williams	34				
7	John	Smith	89				
8	Bob	Clinton	67				
9	Bob	Jones	12				
10	Bob	McCarthy	56				

and elsewhere in your workbook you have a first and last name which you'd like to find the amount value. That is, you have Bob Williams in F2:G2 and you need to pick up the value from cell C6. You can't use any of the LOOKUP functions, and you can't directly use the MATCH function either. What to do?

Formulas

Here, an *array* formula comes to the rescue.

H2	▼	fx	{=INDEX(C:C,MATCH(F2&G2,$A$1:$A$21&$B$1:$B$21,0))}

	A	B	C	D	E	F	G	H	I
1	Master List					Find			
2	First	Last	Amount			Bob	Williams	34	
3	Bob	Smith	23			Fred	Williams	78	
4	Fred	Williams	78			Bob	Clinton	67	
5	Bob	Devon	45						
6	Bob	Williams	34						
7	John	Smith	89						
8	Bob	Clinton	67						
9	Bob	Jones	12						
10	Bob	McCarthy	56						

F2&G2 becomes the string "BobWilliams", and this is being matched against A1:A21&B1:B21 which, when selected in the formula bar and the F9 key is pressed, expands to:

```
=INDEX(C:C,MATCH(F2&G2,{"Master List";"First Last";"BobSmith";"FredWilliams";"BobDevon";"BobWilliams";"JohnSmith";"BobClinton";
"BobJones";"BobMcCarthy";"";"";"";"";"";"";"";"";"";""},0))
```

and you can see that the combination BobWilliams is the 6th item in the list, so this formula reduces to =INDEX(C:C,6), which is C6, so the result 34 is returned.

36. Making exact copies of ranges with relative or mixed references

This technique is useful if you have many cells to copy—otherwise, it's pretty simple to copy the formula directly from the formula bar. Usually, if you copy a range which has relative or mixed references to a new range, the references will adjust. That is, if A1 contains =C7 and you copy A1:B2 to C2:D3, then C2 will contain =E8. Here's how you can have C2 still contain =C7.

We'll use the above references as an example.

To copy A1:B2 to C2:D3 and not change *any* references in the resulting range.

Here's the formulas we're starting with, using relative, mixed, and absolute references:

	A	B
	Book1	
1	=C7	=D$7
2	=$C8	=$D$8

And here's the worksheet displayed normally:

	A	B	C	D
1	abc	def		
2	ghi	jkl		
3				
4				
5				
6				
7			abc	def
8			ghi	jkl

1. Use a 2nd worksheet in group edit mode. To do that Ctrl/click a second (unused) sheet tab:

	A	B	C	D
	Book1 [Group]			
1	abc	def		
2	ghi	jkl		
3				
4				
5				
6				
7			abc	def
8			ghi	jkl
9				
10				

Sheet1 / Sheet2 / Sheet3 /

(Notice both sheets 1 and 2 are selected, and there's another indication you're in group mode—above column A you can see "[Group]".

Formulas

2. Select A1:B2, use Edit/Fill/Across Worksheets (this is dimmed when you're not in group edit mode):

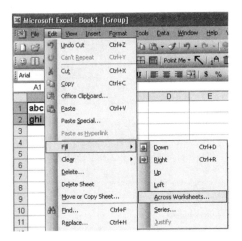

and you're presented with this dialogue:

Now, Sheet2 contains the exact same references in A1:B2 as Sheet1 contains.

3. Activate 2nd worksheet (*not* in group edit)—you do this by Shift/ clicking on Sheet2's tab. Since we didn't copy C7:D8 as well, you only see 0's in Sheet2, but that's fine.

4. In Sheet2, *Cut* A1:B2 and paste to C2:

C2		▼	f_x =C7	
	A	B	C	D
1				
2			0	0
3			0	0

You can see in the formula bar that cell C2 still contains the reference to C7. This is because the references don't change in a cut/paste, only in copy/paste.

5. Back to group edit (with Sheet2 active, Ctrl/click Sheet1), select C2:D3, use Edit/Fill/Across Worksheets, filling 2nd sheet back to first. Shift/click Sheet1 and you'll see:

C2		▼	*fx* =C7	
	A	B	C	D
1	abc	def		
2	ghi	jkl	abc	def
3			ghi	jkl
4				
5				
6				
7			abc	def
8			ghi	jkl

– the formulas are:

	A	B	C	D
1	=C7	=D$7		
2	=$C8	=$D$8	=C7	=D$7
3			=$C8	=$D$8

Formulas

37. Named ranges which define themselves

Currently you have Database defined as $A$1:$E$25.

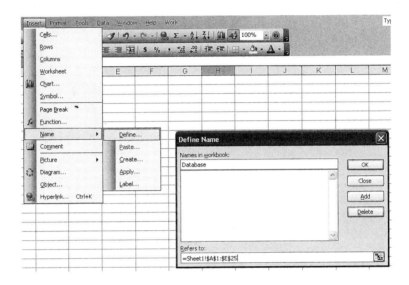

You add a record to row 26, and then need to redefine the range to include the new row.

Assuming there are no "holes" in the first column of the database, change the definition to be =OFFSET($A$1,0,0,COUNTA($A:$A),5). This means starting with cell A1, 0 rows down and 0 columns over, in COUNTA(A:A) rows by 5 columns. (COUNTA returns the number of non-blank cells).

This automatically will include new rows added because the COUNTA result will change. If it were now A1:E25, then the COUNTA function returns 25. When you add a new record, the COUNTA returns 26, so the new definition is =OFFSET(A1,0,0,26,5), or A1:E26.

Formulas

38. *Using REPT for visual effects*

You can easily use a variation on =REPT("∧",500) for a nice effect (that's a / followed by a \). Shown below, you can see the effect of the formula entered in cell A1.

	A	B	C	D	E	F	G
	A1	▼	fx	=REPT("∧",500)			
1	∿∿∿						
2	==						
3	[-][-						
4	<><><><><><><><><><><><><><><><><><><><><><><><						
5							

Cell A2 contains =REPT("=",500).
Cell A3 contains =REPT("[-]",500).
Cell A4 contains =REPT("<>",500).

Go be creative!

39. *Using the Space as an operator*

The space is as valid an operator as +, -, /, or *.
=West Gizmos will pick up the intersection of the 2 ranges, West and Gizmos:

	A	B	C	D	E
	C9	▼	fx	=West Gizmos	
		North	West	South	East
1					
2	Things	24	51	92	91
3	Gizmos	37	85	39	98
4	Objects	53	74	58	8
5					
6					
7					
8					
9			85		

Here, West is defined as C2:C4, and Gizmos as B3:E3. They intersect in C3, which is the result you see in cell C9. The space operator is an intersection operation.

Formulas

40. Extracting the last part of a string

Suppose you have this in a cell: C:\MSOFFICE\EXCEL\LIBRARY\MS-QUERY\MyFile.xls, and you'd like to pick out the last piece, MyFile. xls. Here's how to do it.

The technique basically changes the *last* slash to some unique character, then finds where that character is, and returns from that position + 1 to the end.

First, there are a few things you need to know. There's a LEN function which returns the number of characters in a string, or cell. So if A1 contains ABCA, =LEN(A1) would return 4.

The SUBSTITUTE function substitutes one value for another in a cell. So =SUBSTITUTE(A1,"C","Q") would return ABQA in the above example.

Also, =SUBSTITUTE(A1,"A","Q") would return QBCQ, because it changes *both* A's. We're going to take advantage of another option in the SUBSTITUTE function, where we can change a *particular* occurrence.
=SUBSTITUTE(A1,"A","Q",1) would give QBCA, and
=SUBSTITUTE(A1,"A","Q",2) would give ABCQ. The 1 and 2 tells which one to change.

Okay, preliminaries are done. Let's go back to where A1 contains C:\MSOFFICE\EXCEL\LIBRARY\MSQUERY\MyFile.xls.

1. =LEN(A1) is 44.

2. =SUBSTITUTE(A1, "\"", "") is C:MSOFFICEEXCELLIBRARYMS-QUERYMyFile.xls—the same string without the backslashes.

3. That length (LEN(SUBSTITUTE(A1, "\"", "") is 39.

4. =LEN(A1)-LEN(SUBSTITUTE(A1,"\","")) is 5, telling us there are 5 backslashes. If we use *that* as the 4th parameter in the SUBSTITUTE function, we will only change the 5th slash.

5. =SUBSTITUTE(A1,"\",CHAR(222),*the value from step 4*) changes the last backslash to a CHAR(222). (CHAR(222) is kind of arbitrary strange character…hang in there!)

6. =FIND(CHAR(222), *the value from step 5*) finds what position that character is in—that is, where the last slash is!

7. =MID(A1,*the value from step 6*+1,255) gives just MyFile.xls.
Putting it all together:
=MID(A1,SEARCH(CHAR(222),SUBSTITUTE(A1,"\ ",CHAR(222),LEN(A1)-LEN(SUBSTITUTE(A1,"\","")))))+1,255) will return MyFile.xls.

A2	▼	*fx*	=MID(A1,SEARCH(CHAR(222),SUBSTITUTE(A1,"\",CHAR(222), LEN(A1)-LEN(SUBSTITUTE(A1,"\","")))))+1,255)
1	C:\MSOFFICE\EXCEL\LIBRARY\MSQUERY\MyFile.xls		
2	MyFile.xls		

41. Using SUMPRODUCT

Instead of trying to make SUMIF or COUNTIF work on multiple conditions (you can't), use SUMPRODUCT.

Look at the following worksheet:

	A	B	C	D	E	F	G	H	I
1	Years	Names	Amts						
2	2003	Fred	1						
3	2004	Bob	2						
4	2001	Fred	3	11					
5	2003	Fred	4	=SUMPRODUCT((A2:A11=2004)*(B2:B11="Bob")*C2:C11)					
6	2004	Fred	5						
7	2004	Fred	6	2					
8	2003	Bob	7	=SUMPRODUCT((A2:A11=2004)*(B2:B11="Bob"))					
9	2001	Fred	8						
10	2004	Bob	9	11					
11	2003	Fred	10	=SUMPRODUCT(--(A2:A11=2004),--(B2:B11="Bob"),--C2:C11)					

Cell D4, which contains the formula shown in D5, returns 11. This is the sum of the amounts in column C which correspond to the year being 2004 and the name being Bob. That occurs only in rows 3 and 10. The formula works like this: The part of the formula which is A2:A11=2004 evaluates to (what you'd see if you selected that part of the formula and pressed F9):
    {FALSE;TRUE;FALSE;FALSE;TRUE;TRUE;FALSE;FALSE;TRUE;FALSE}
Where the TRUE's correspond to the 2004's. B2:B11="Bob" evaluates to:

{FALSE;TRUE;FALSE;FALSE;FALSE;FALSE;TRUE;FALSE;TRUE;FALSE}.

Now these are being multiplied together. Only TRUE * TRUE is 1, any other combination is 0. (You can try it in a cell—enter =FALSE*TRUE, for example). So this produces {0,1,0,0,0,0,0,0,1,0}, where the 1's correspond to a *pair* of TRUE's. Now this in turn is multiplied by the range in C2:C11, or {1;2;3;4;5;6;7;8;9;10}. This multiplication yields {0;2;0;0;0;0;0;0;9;0}, and this is added up to produce the 11.

Cell D7 (formula shown in D8) only returns the {0;1;0;0;0;0;0;0;1;0} part of the multiplication, and this is added up to produce the 2— which represents a COUNT of the number of records for which the year is 2004 and the name is Bob.

You may have seen another variation of the formula in cell D4. Cell D10 contains the formula shown in D11. What is the "--" before each set of parentheses? If you enter =-TRUE in a cell, you'll see -1, =-FALSE yields 0. so --TRUE yields 1, and --FALSE still yields 0. The -- coerces the set of TRUE/FALSEs shown above to 1's & 0's (not -1's & 0's). so the formula really reduces to =SUMPROD-UCT({0;1;0;0;1;1;0;0;1;0},{0;1;0;0;0;0;1;0;1;0},{1;2;3;4;5;6;7;8;9;10}) which again becomes SUMPRODUCT({0;2;0;0;0;0;0;0;9;0}), or 11.

42. *Using the TEXT function*

Date won't fit in column?

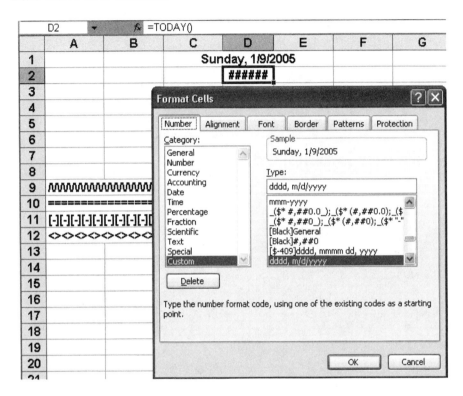

Cell D2 contains =TODAY() and is formatted as shown: dddd, m/d/ yyyy. Well, it won't fit. If you're restricted from changing the column width, what can you do? The solution is the TEXT function. Cell D1 contains this formula: =TEXT(TODAY(),"dddd, m/d/yyyy")

Since this returns text, it will flow into the next column if there's not enough room to display in its own column.

43. Allow only unique entries in a column

Use Data/Validation with a custom formula like
=COUNTIF(B:B.B1)=1:

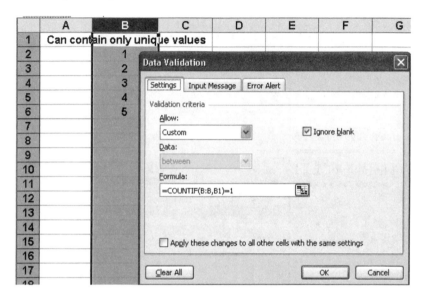

Remember the COUNTIF function—its syntax is =COUNTIF(Range, criteria). With all the cells in column B selected, this formula returns TRUE only if the COUNTIF for all of column B (the range) contains only 1 value of "Can contain only unique values". If you were to select B2 at this point and re-examine the data validation formula, you'd see =COUNTIF(B:B,B2)=1.

Let's enter 1 in cell B7 and see what happens:

	A	B	C	D
1	Can contain only unique values			
2		1		
3		2		
4		3		
5		4		
6		5		
7		1		
8				
9		Microsoft Excel ✕		
10				
11		This value has already been entered!		
12				
13		Retry Cancel		

The message appears because the data validation for cell B7 is =COUNTIF(B:B,B7), which returns 2. The message comes from the error alert tab of the Data/Validation dialog:

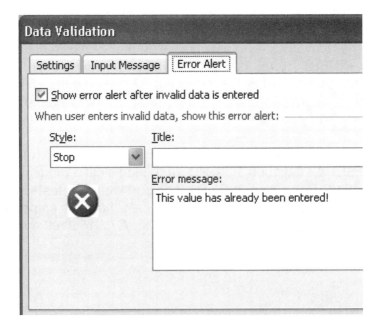

Formulas

44. Use wildcards in MATCH function

Look at this worksheet:

	C2	▼	*fx*	=B2/INDEX(B:B,MATCH("*Total",OFFSET(A2,0,0,1000,1),0)+ROW()-1)		
[1][2][3]		**A**	**B**	**C**	**D**	**E**	**F**

	A	B	C	D	E	F
1	Dept	Amt	% of Total			
2	Dept1	872	30%			
3	Dept1	869	30%			
4	Dept1	384	13%			
5	Dept1	794	27%			
6	Dept1 Total	2919	100%			
7	Dept2	340	10%			
8	Dept2	762	23%			
9	Dept2	426	13%			
10	Dept2	367	11%			
11	Dept2	207	6%			
12	Dept2	122	4%			
13	Dept2	564	17%			
14	Dept2	459	14%			
15	Dept2 Total	3247	100%			
16	Dept3	671	4%			

The formula in C2 is filled down as far as necessary (past C16) and yet it returns the percent each number in column B is to the total value *for that department*. It's based on the fact that the total is indicated in column A by text ending in the word "Total".

Part of the formula uses an asterisk inside the MATCH function: =MATCH("*Total",... will look for anything *ending* in the word Total (case *in*sensitive). So, cell C2 is dividing B2 by that number in column B which corresponds to the next Total, or in this example, it's B2 divided by B6.

Let's examine the formula more closely. =B2/INDEX(B:B,MATCH("*Total",OFFSET(A2,0,0,1000,1),0)+ROW()-1) in this case winds up being =B2/INDEX(B:B,6), which is B2/B6. The part we're interested in here is how the 6 is derived. And more specifically, how this same formula in C3 through C6 returns 6 and how in cells C7:C15 it returns 15.

Formulas

Okay, back to cell C2. =MATCH("*Total",OFFSET(A2,0,0,1000,1),0) is the same as =MATCH("*Total",A2:A1001,0) because the OFFSET function as used here says to start with A2, go 0 rows down and 0 columns over, and use a shape of 1000 rows x 1 column, or A2:A1001. This part returns 5 because the MATCH function never returns 0—it's a value from 1 and up, or #N/A if not found. An adjustment needs to be made. We *need* 6, so we can just add 1! But that seems like cheating. And in C3, the MATCH would return 4 and adding 1 wouldn't be right; we'd need to add 2! In other words, we need to add one less than the row the formula is contained in: in C2 add 1; in C3 add 2, in C4 add 3. So in cell Cn, add n-1. Now look at the formula. We're adding ROW()-1.

I've added a column in this next illustration which is simply the part of the formula from the MATCH on:

	D7	▼	fx =MATCH("*Total",OFFSET(A7,0,0,1000,1),0)+ROW()-1		
1 2 3		A	B	C	D	E
	1	Dept	Amt	% of Total		
	2	Dept1	872	30%	6	
	3	Dept1	869	30%	6	
	4	Dept1	384	13%	6	
	5	Dept1	794	27%	6	
	6	Dept1 Total	2919	100%	6	
	7	Dept2	340	10%	15	
	8	Dept2	762	23%	15	
	9	Dept2	426	13%	15	
	10	Dept2	367	11%	15	
	11	Dept2	207	6%	15	
	12	Dept2	122	4%	15	
	13	Dept2	564	17%	15	
	14	Dept2	459	14%	15	
	15	Dept2 Total	3247	100%	15	

What makes this formula interesting is that it can be filled down as far as necessary without knowing what row the total is in.

Formulas

45. Right-mouse/drag the border of a range for several new options

If you right-mouse drag and drop the *border* of a range to a new location, then when you let go of the right-click, you're presented with a dialog containing many options:

	A	B	C	D
1	36	45	1/1/2003	
2	40	50	2/1/2003	
3				
4				
5			Move Here	
6			Copy Here	
7			Copy Here as Values Only	
8			Copy Here as Formats Only	
9				
10			Link Here	
11			Create Hyperlink Here	
12			Shift Down and Copy	
13			Shift Right and Copy	
14			Shift Down and Move	
15			Shift Right and Move	
16			Cancel	
17				

If you drag a range this way and before letting go you drag it right back to the original location, you will still be presented with the above dialog, and this way you can copy/paste special values in place with the mouse.

46. Ctrl/Shift/~,1,2,3,4,5,6 for quick formatting

These simply keyboard shortcuts can help with number formatting (here, the value 1.5 was entered in the cell):

Ctrl+Shift+:	Resulting Format:	Example:
~	General	1.5
1	2 decimals	1.50
2	Time format	12:00 PM
3	Date format	1-Jan-00
4	Currency	$1.50
5	Percent	150%
6	Scientific	1.50E+00

47. Borders from keyboard

Ctrl/Shift/7 creates outline border
Ctrl/Shift/- removes border

On the Macintosh, use Option/Command keys instead of Ctrl/Shift keys.

48. Inserting Date & Time shortcuts

Ctrl/Semicolon (Ctrl/;) will insert the date in m/d/yyyy format;
Ctrl/Colon (Ctrl/:) will insert the time in h:mm AM/PM format.

49. Shift/click inner VCR controls

In the tab VCR-type scrolling controls,

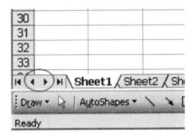

if you hold the Shift key down while clicking one of the inner two controls, you will scroll a "page" of tabs (all the tabs that are viewable) at a time instead of one sheet at a time.

50. Click the AutoSum button from the keyboard

Alt/= is the same as clicking the AutoSum tool.
Alt/= twice (quickly) will also *enter* the result.

51. Bringing the selection into view

It's possible you've selected some area of cells and then scrolled away so you can't see it anymore. Ctrl/Backspace brings that selection into view, and Shift/backspace brings selection into view as well but reduces the selection to the active cell. So, if this is the before picture:

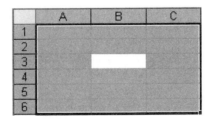

then Shift/backspace will simply have cell B3 selected.

52. Ctrl/[more powerful than its "equivalent" Go to Precedents

If a cell has =SUM(B2:E4), then with that cell selected, use Edit/Go to Special and select Precedents. The result is that cells B2:E4 will be selected.

Ctrl/[does the same thing.

However, if a cell has a link to a cell in a closed workbook (the entire path would be shown in the cell), then using Edit/Go to Special would give an error message:

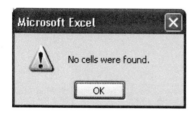

whereas Ctrl/[would open the file, switch to the appropriate sheet, and select the cell.

The Go to/Special dialog also has an "All levels" option button when you select Precedents (or Dependents). This means that if, in the first example above, cell C3 had a formula which referenced H12, the all-levels option would also select cell H12 (in addition to B2:E4).

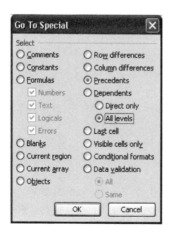

The equivalent keyboard shortcut is Ctrl/Shift/[.

53. Ctrl/6 is a 3-way toggle

Same as Tools/Options/View and choosing between:
• Show All
• Show Placeholders
• Hide All

(It's *not* Ctrl/F6, but Ctrl/6).

The above is for showing or hiding objects, including charts. Doing so makes it a lot quicker for scrolling, especially if there are many charts because the screen doesn't have to redraw while you scroll.
It can also reveal cells that are hidden by objects.

Show Placeholders works for charts only, not other objects. Here's a worksheet with Show All:

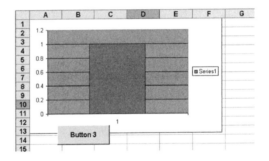

And here is the same with Show Placeholders:

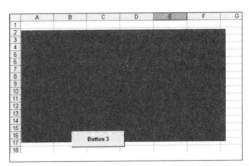

By the way, if you have Hide All as the option, all drawing objects are disabled, and trying to create a chart will automatically go onto its own sheet, not as an embedded chart.
Just use Ctrl/6.

54. Show corners of selection easily

Ctrl/period successively selects corners of the selection, even if the entire selection is large, as in A1:DD799.

55. Copy Page Setups to other sheets

If sheet1 has the setup you want and sheet2 is to receive the same settings:

Here's what the print preview looks like for sheet1:

And sheet2:

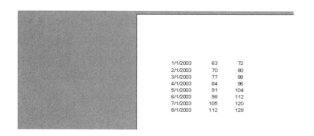

So, you can see that sheet2 is portrait and has no left/center header, while sheet1 has landscape, has an italicized center header, a date for the left header, and the data is shown with gridlines and row & column headings. We'd like sheet2's settings to be the same as sheet1's settings. Here's how to do it:

1. Put both sheets in group edit (with sheet1 active, Ctrl/click sheet2—*you can also Shift/click, but if you're using sheets which aren't next to each other, Ctrl/click will only put the 2nd sheet in group mode, whereas Shift/click will put all the sheets in-between in group mode*).

Keyboard Shortcuts/Printing

2. Use File/Page Setup

3. Click OK (you don't even have to look at the settings!)

4. Get out of group edit (Shift click a sheet tab)

5. That's it. Really! Here's Sheet2 now:

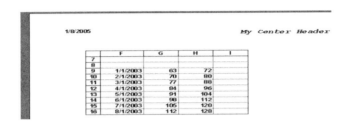

You can do this with >1 sheet at a time, or even the entire workbook. To do it for more than 1 sheet, simply put all the sheets in group mode and have the sheet with the settings you want to copy be the active sheet. Then Page setup/OK/get out of group mode.

To do the entire workbook, right-click a sheet tab, select "Select All Sheets", and repeat the process.

Don't forget to get out of group mode!

56. Copy Page Setups across workbooks

You *can* temporarily copy in the sheet from the desired settings to the second workbook and proceed as in the previous tip.

But this method brings in names, styles, number formats, and links as well. Here's another approach which avoids that problem.

Using VBA, run this command:
Application.Dialogs(xlDialogWorkgroup).Show. This puts all open workbooks and worksheets in group edit mode.

With workbooks Book1 and Book4 open, that produces this dialog:

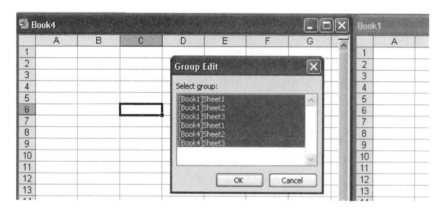

Selecting the sheets which contain the page setups to be copied, you can then simply issue the File/Page Setup command as before. Once again, make sure that the sheet with the proper Page Setup is the active sheet, because selecting any other sheet will take you out of group mode.

And, once again, don't forget to get out of group edit mode.

57. Print many worksheets at once

To do this, just put them in group mode:
Right-click sheet tab & choose "Select All Sheets":

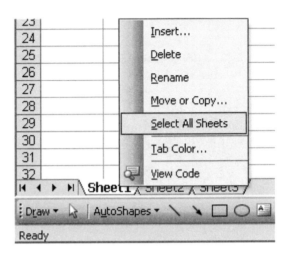

Or Ctrl/click specific sheets to print.
Then Print!

Don't forget to take the sheets out of group mode, which you can do by Shift/clicking any sheet.

58. Clear all page breaks

Insert Page Break becomes Reset All Page Breaks when all the cells are selected (if there are manual page breaks).

Note, however, that if you have a Page Setup which includes a setting like Adjust to 80% normal size, this also gets reset to 100% by the Reset All Page Breaks command.

Not nice!

Printing

59. Print remote areas on same page

To do this, use the camera tool. You can get it by View/Toolbars/Customize, click on the Commands tab, then select the Tools Category and the Camera tool is about 3/4 of the way down (varies with the version of Excel). Drag this tool to a toolbar.

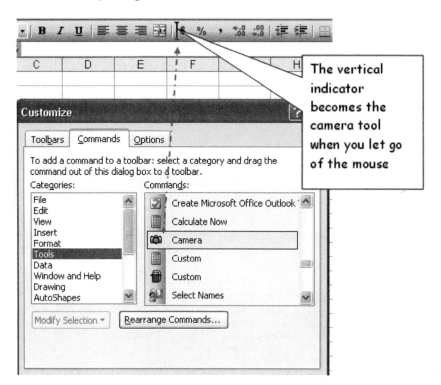

The vertical indicator becomes the camera tool when you let go of the mouse

Next, select the remote cells, and click camera tool.

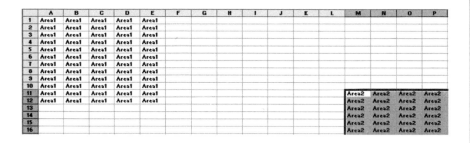

"Develop" the picture near the original range by clicking where you want the picture to go.

Picture 5	▼		*fx*	=$M$11:$R$19	
	A	**B**	**C**	**D**	**E**	**F**
1	Area1	Area1	Area1	Area1	Area1	
2	Area1	Area1	Area1	Area1	Area1	
3	Area1	Area1	Area1	Area1	Area1	
4	Area1	Area1	Area1	Area1	Area1	
5	Area1	Area1	Area1	Area1	Area1	
6	Area1	Area1	Area1	Area1	Area1	
7	Area1	Area1	Area1	Area1	Area1	
8	Area1	Area1	Area1	Area1	Area1	
9	Area1	Area1	Area1	Area1	Area1	
10	Area1	Area1	Area1	Area1	Area1	
11	Area1	Area1	Area1	Area1	Area1	
12	Area1	Area1	Area1	Area1	Area1	
13	Area2	Area2	Area2	Area2	Area2	Area2
14	Area2	Area2	Area2	Area2	Area2	Area2
15	Area2	Area2	Area2	Area2	Area2	Area2
16	Area2	Area2	Area2	Area2	Area2	Area2
17	Area2	Area2	Area2	Area2	Area2	Area2
18	Area2	Area2	Area2	Area2	Area2	Area2
19	Area2	Area2	Area2	Area2	Area2	Area2
20	Area2	Area2	Area2	Area2	Area2	Area2
21	Area2	Area2	Area2	Area2	Area2	Area2

If you hold the Alt key, the picture will exactly line up with the closest cell grid.

For best results, you want to turn off the gridlines and remove the border after the picture is shown. (Note the address in the formula bar.)

	A	**B**	**C**	**D**	**E**	**F**
1	Area1	Area1	Area1	Area1	Area1	
2	Area1	Area1	Area1	Area1	Area1	
3	Area1	Area1	Area1	Area1	Area1	
4	Area1	Area1	Area1	Area1	Area1	
5	Area1	Area1	Area1	Area1	Area1	
6	Area1	Area1	Area1	Area1	Area1	
7	Area1	Area1	Area1	Area1	Area1	
8	Area1	Area1	Area1	Area1	Area1	
9	Area1	Area1	Area1	Area1	Area1	
10	Area1	Area1	Area1	Area1	Area1	
11	Area1	Area1	Area1	Area1	Area1	
12	Area1	Area1	Area1	Area1	Area1	
13	Area2	Area2	Area2	Area2	Area2	Area2
14	Area2	Area2	Area2	Area2	Area2	Area2
15	Area2	Area2	Area2	Area2	Area2	Area2
16	Area2	Area2	Area2	Area2	Area2	Area2
17	Area2	Area2	Area2	Area2	Area2	Area2
18	Area2	Area2	Area2	Area2	Area2	Area2
19	Area2	Area2	Area2	Area2	Area2	Area2
20	Area2	Area2	Area2	Area2	Area2	Area2
21	Area2	Area2	Area2	Area2	Area2	Area2

Now select the cells to print, including the cells "behind" the picture and set the print area, then print. It will print on one page instead of one page for each remote area.

60. Anchoring the active cell

Holding the Shift key down while you click a cell, or double-click a border, or even in the Edit/Go to dialog (F5) will keep that cell as the active cell.

If cell C4 is active, as shown, and you use the Edit/Go to dialog and enter e9 as the cell to go to:

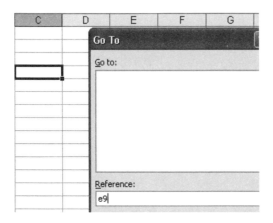

then if you hold the Shift key down when you click the OK button, this will be your result:

In other words, the original active cell will still be the active cell.

If you Shift click cell A2, now, the selection will be A2:C4, with C4 being the active cell.

Since Ctrl/down arrow (or right/left/up arrow) takes you to the end of a block, *Shift*/Ctrl/arrow will also take you to the end of the block, but the active cell won't change.

61. Filling holes

Suppose you have a worksheet something like this:

	A	B	C
1	State	Region	Amount
2	PA	North	300
3			104
4			159
5			749
6		South	700
7			348
8			508
9			935
10			582
11	WA	North	377
12			936
13		South	831
14			243
15			344
16	NY	North	97
17			120
18		South	577
19			955

And you'd like to sort it by state! Yikes. You KNOW it would be quite messed up because of the holes (empty cells). In this example it wouldn't take *too* long to fill PA down from A2:A10, then WA from A11 to A15, etc. and then it'd be easy to sort, but if this extended to row 6000, forget it.

Well, there's an easy way:

1. Select cells, use Edit/Go To click Special, select Blanks:

	A	B	C
1	State	Region	Amount
2	PA	North	300
3			104
4			159
5			749
6		South	700
7			348
8			508
9			935
10			582
11	WA	North	377
12			936
13		South	831
14			243
15			344
16	NY	North	97
17			120
18		South	577
19			955

2. Type "=", press the up-arrow, then press Ctrl/Enter:

	B3	▼	fx =B2	
	A	B	C	
1	State	Region	Amount
2	PA	North	300
3	PA	North	104
4	PA	North	159
5	PA	North	749
6	PA	South	700
7	PA	South	348
8	PA	South	508
9	PA	South	935
10	PA	South	582
11	WA	North	377
12	WA	North	936
13	WA	South	831
14	WA	South	243
15	WA	South	344
16	NY	North	97
17	NY	North	120
18	NY	South	577
19	NY	South	955

What? It can't be that easy! What happened? Look at cell B3: It says =B2, or *the cell above*. Ctrl/Enter says "fill the selected cells with the formula", so every blank cell references the cell above. So A12 says =A11, etc.

Miscellaneous

Now the sort is trivial. And if you want to clear the formulas, simply select 1 cell, use Edit/Go To click Special, select Formulas & OK, then press the delete key to produce the sorted result.

	A	B	C
1	State	Region	Amount
2	NY	North	97
3			120
4		South	577
5			955
6	PA	North	300
7			104
8			159
9			749
10		South	700
11			348
12			508
13			935
14			582
15	WA	North	377
16			936
17		South	831
18			243
19			344

Miscellaneous

62. *Using pictographs*

Anything in the clipboard can be pasted onto a chart:

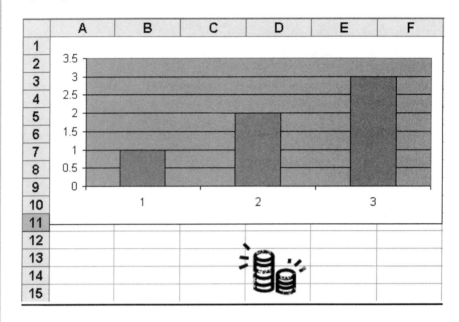

Clicking on the coins, edit/copy, click on a series, edit paste:

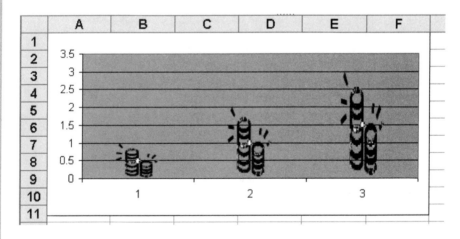

Click on the series, use Format/Selected Data Series:

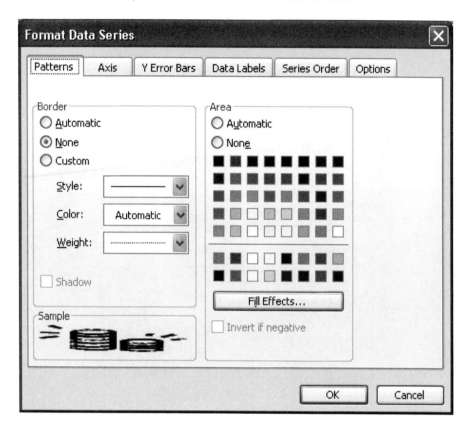

Click the Fill Effects button (slightly different location on a Macintosh—you need to select it from the color dropdown):

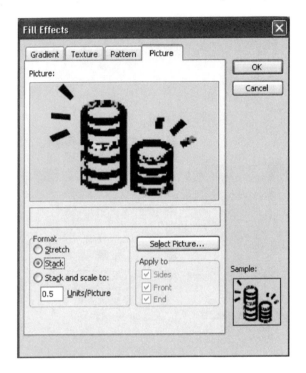

There are 3 format options:
1. Stretch (default)
2. Stack
3. Stack and scale to

If we select Stack, we see:

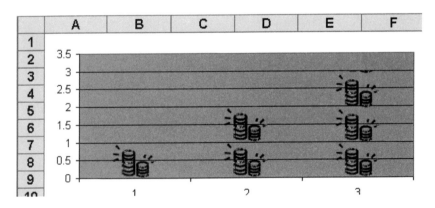

If we select Stack and scale, we can enter a number into the Unit/ Picture box. Again, this is something you can experiment with.

You also may have noticed the tabs in this dialog:
• Gradient
• Texture
• Pattern
• Picture (the one we got by default)

Here's the gradient tab:

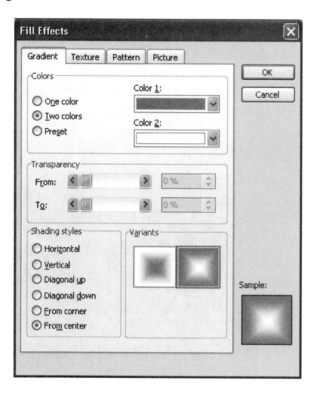

On the picture tab there was a button to select a picture—you can use any picture you have on your computer.

You can experiment with the other tabs as well.

63. See all characters in font set

1. Enter =CHAR(ROW()) in row 1
   a. =ROW() returns the row you're in. =ROW() entered in cell G23 returns 23.
   b. =CHAR(97) returns the 97th character in the character set for that font, usually a lowercase "a". (picture fonts like Wingdings or Webdings return something else).
2. Fill down to row 255
3. Easy to see things like •, ¢, £:

	A
147	"
148	"
149	•
150	–
151	—
152	˜
153	TM
154	š
155	›
156	œ
157	□
158	ž
159	Ÿ
160	
161	¡
162	¢
163	£

When you see that "•" is in row 149, you can then know that holding Alt while typing 0149 on the numeric keypad will create this character, as soon as you let go of the Alt key. This part doesn't apply to the Macintosh—you'd need to use the CHAR function. You can copy/paste special values for the character(s) you want, and you can then copy the resulting character from the formula bar. The leading 0 is necessary.

64. Aligning objects

The draw menu of the Drawing toolbar has this feature:

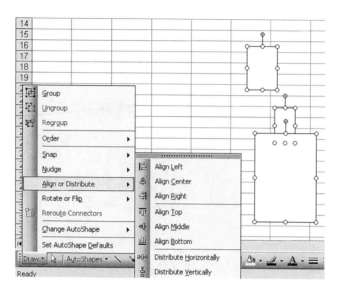

For example, if you use Distribute Vertically on the left worksheet with the objects selected…and you'll see the right worksheet:

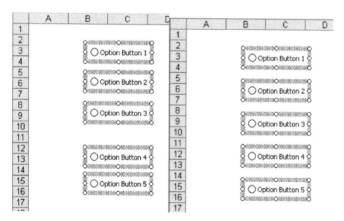

65. Wish there were a "No to All" when closing many files?

There is!

Hold the Shift key when clicking the No button and you won't be prompted to save changes on any workbook.

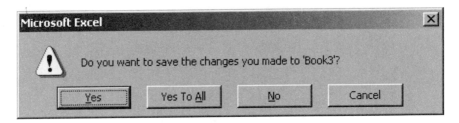

66. Leaving cursor in the cell after pressing enter

If the cursor normally moves out of the cell when you enter a value and you temporarily want to keep it in the same cell, simply press Ctrl/enter instead of enter.

Assumes you have only 1 cell selected, otherwise *all* the cells will be filled!

67. Deleting Print Area

The print area, if set, is a defined name: "Print_Area". There are many ways to delete it.

1. Insert/Name/Define, and delete it is one way:

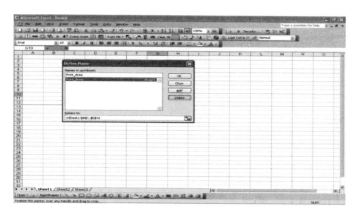

If you happen to have hundreds (or thousands) of names defined, you don't have to *scroll* to the name to delete it, you can simply type the name and click the Delete button. So this isn't really only for Print_ Area—it works for any defined name. A *very* useful utility for managing defined names, developed by fellow MVP Jan Karel Pieterse, can be downloaded from http://www.decisionmodels.com/Downloads. htm#namemanager.

2. If you have the "Set Print Area" toolbar button, you can select all the cells and click the button. There are a few ways to select all the cells:
    a. Select all cells with Ctrl/Shift/Spacebar
    b. Select all cells by clicking the empty box above row #1 and to the left of column A.
    c. Press Ctrl/A twice (twice depending on the version of Excel you have—maybe once will do!)

If you don't have the Set Print Area toolbar button, here's how you can get it (it's a pretty nice time-saver, not just for *deleting* the print area, but for setting it!)
    a. Use View/Toolbars/Customize
    b. Click the Commands tab

Miscellaneous

3. On the file category, scroll to the Set Print Area toolbar:

4. Drag it into the toolbar where you want (I keep mine near the Print toolbar button):

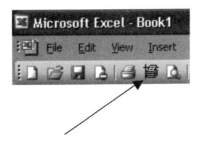

68. Double-spacing data

Here's a technique to double-space your data which is faster than any macro could do it (unless the macro utilizes this technique also!) Imagine being able to double-space thousands of rows in a split second. The secret? Sort them.

1. Number the rows. In this example the data is in A1:D9. We used column E for the row numbering:

	A	B	C	D	E	F	G	H
1	Data	Data	Data	Data	1			
2	Data	Data	Data	Data	2			
3	Data	Data	Data	Data	3			
4	Data	Data	Data	Data	4			
5	Data	Data	Data	Data	5			
6	Data	Data	Data	Data	6			
7	Data	Data	Data	Data	7			
8	Data	Data	Data	Data	8			
9	Data	Data	Data	Data	9			

the rows -- enter 1 in E1, 2 in E2. Select E1:E2, double-click the fill handle

2. Copy and paste these numbers so there are 2 sets

	A	B	C	D	E
1	Data	Data	Data	Data	1
2	Data	Data	Data	Data	2
3	Data	Data	Data	Data	3
4	Data	Data	Data	Data	4
5	Data	Data	Data	Data	5
6	Data	Data	Data	Data	6
7	Data	Data	Data	Data	7
8	Data	Data	Data	Data	8
9	Data	Data	Data	Data	9
10					1
11					2
12					3
13					4
14					5
15					6
16					7
17					8
18					9

Miscellaneous

3. Sort the data by this column. This sorts the blank rows into their correct place.

	A	B	C	D	E
Book1					
1	Data	Data	Data	Data	1
2					1
3	Data	Data	Data	Data	2
4					2
5	Data	Data	Data	Data	3
6					3
7	Data	Data	Data	Data	4
8					4
9	Data	Data	Data	Data	5
10					5
11	Data	Data	Data	Data	6
12					6
13	Data	Data	Data	Data	7
14					7
15	Data	Data	Data	Data	8
16					8
17	Data	Data	Data	Data	9
18					9

4. Clear the column, and you're done. You can use this technique to triple-space by pasting another set of row #s before the sort.

69. *Quick return from Edit/Go to...*

The "return" address of the last range you visited via another Edit/Go to is stored in the Go to dialog, so to return quickly, use the F5 key and press Enter. Actually, the last 4 addresses you've gone to are kept.

70. *Using fills*

A number format which includes * will fill the cell with the *next* character. A format of General*. will fill the cell with periods. Enter 12 and you'll see 12.............. as wide as the column is:

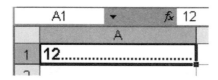

Use a format of $**#,##0 to get asterisk-fill for currency. The first * is the code indicating to use the *next* character to fill the cell. *That* next character is *, so now 12 looks like this:

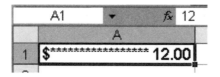

Miscellaneous

71. Fill "=A1" right, have reference become =A2, =A3, ...

You've probably wanted to be able to fill a formula horizontally and have the resulting formula reference a vertical range. That is, you may have entered =A1, and wanted to fill that to the right but have the result become =A2, =A3, etc. Of course, Excel gives you =B1, =C1, etc.

This is *not* a substitute for either the Transpose function or copy/ Paste Special and checking the Transpose checkbox. We want a dynamic and simple formula reference as a result.

Here's a technique that shows you how to do this.

1. Enter first formula without "=". Here, B2 was entered in cell B12. The B2 is used because that's where the data starts.

	A	B
1		
2		Here's
3		the
4		information
5		to
6		see
7		left
8		to
9		right
10		
11		
12		B2

2. Fill right with the fill handle (You'll have B3, B4, B5,...)

B	C	D	E
Here's			
the			
information			
to			
see			
left			
to			
right			
B2	B3	B4	B5

3. Replace "B" with "=B"

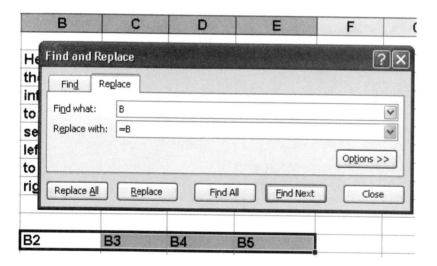

4. Here's the result:

B	C	D	E
Here's			
the			
information			
to			
see			
left			
to			
right			
Here's	the	informatio	to

72. Fill "=C3" down, have reference become =D3, =E3, etc.

This is similar to the preceding tip, but the orientation is the reverse. However, this is a lot trickier. If we enter C3 (without the equal sign) and fill down, we'd get C4, C5, etc, the same as if the equal sign were present. We really want the C to become D, E, etc. Here's how:

1. Enter first formula without "=" *but in R1C1 notation* so instead of =C3, use r3c3, which means row 3, column 3.

C	D	E	F	G	H	I	J
Here's	the	info	to	see	left	to	right
r3c3							

2. Fill down, giving r3c4, r3c5, etc.

C	D	E	F	G	H	I	J
Here's	the	info	to	see	left	to	right
r3c3							
r3c4							
r3c5							
r3c6							
r3c7							

Miscellaneous

3. Switch to R1C1 notation via tools/options/General tab.

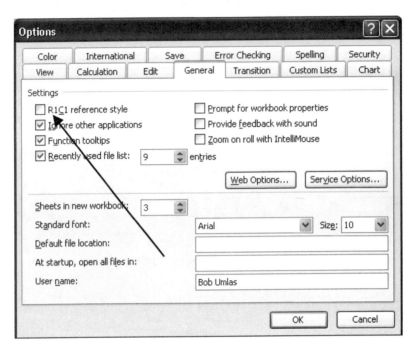

—This step is necessary, because you can't replace r with =r in the above because Excel will give you an error message:

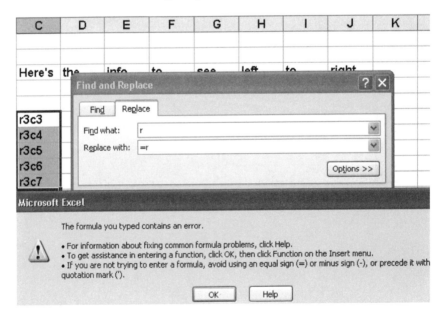

Miscellaneous

4. Replace "r" with "=r" (after switching to R1C1 notation as indicated above).

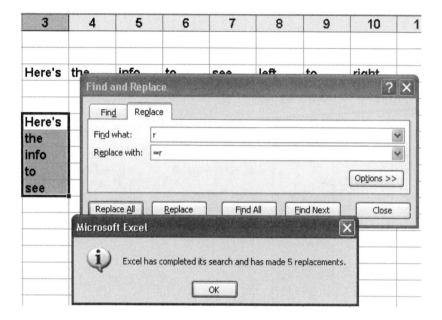

5. Switch back to A1 notation—*un*check the R1C1 notation box in Tools/Options/General tab.

73. "Fun" tip—make your IT person scratch his head!

Enter =NA() in D1, leave D2 blank.
Select D1:D2, use fill handle, drag to D100
Select column D, use Edit/Go to Special, select Formulas, and leave only Errors selected (every odd row will be selected).

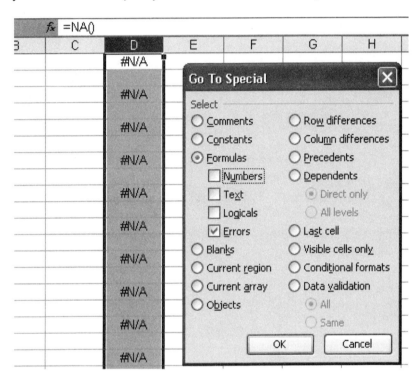

Change font to 100-pt.

Clear contents of column D.

Reset column width of D and make all row heights 12.75:

Where are the odd row#s?

74. *Using Insert/Name/Define and scrolling*

While the Insert/Name/Define dialog is showing you can't scroll unless the cursor is in the refers-to box. Just thought you'd like to know.

75. *Show a picture by typing its name?*

First, let me demo what we're about to accomplish:
I type the word dog in cell A1 and see:

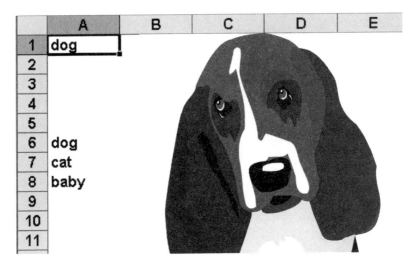

I type cat and see:

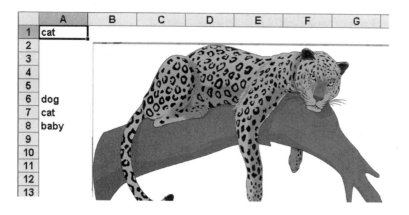

I type baby and see:

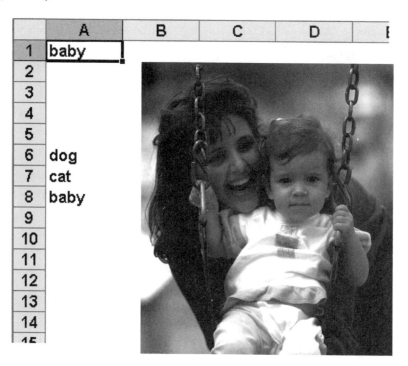

The really neat part is that this is done without macros of any sort, just formulas. Imagine having a parts inventory and being able to type in the part # and get a picture.

Here's how it's done. The pictures need to already exist in the work-sheet and be equally spaced (and out of sight)—here's a 25% view of the worksheet from cell U1:

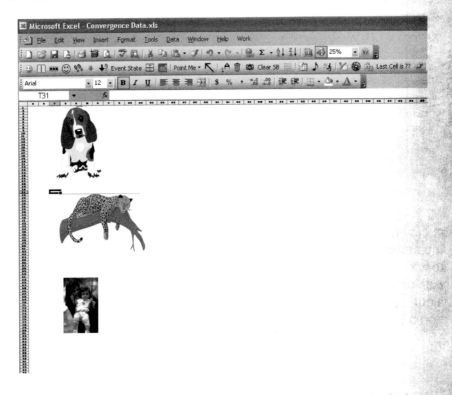

The dog starts in U1, the cat (ok, tiger) starts in U31, and the baby picture in U61. That is, all the pictures here are 30 rows apart.

Next, you need a camera-tool type object whose reference is a defined name, like =pic. The camera tool is found by using View/Toolbars/Customize like this:

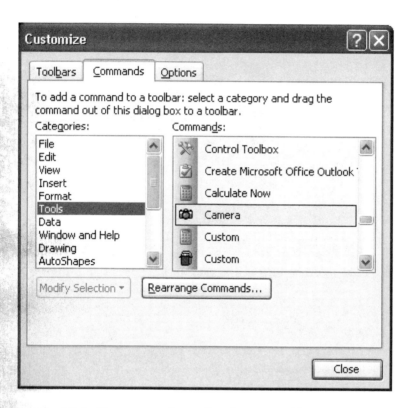

You may find it further up or down the Commands listbox with versions of Excel other than 2003. Here, you can see it's about 2/3 the way down. Drag this to a toolbar of your choice. Then, select a 30 row x 15 column set of cells near column U—like U1:AI30, then click the camera tool. Then click again near where you want the picture to show up. In our example, that was around cell B2.

You should see something like this:

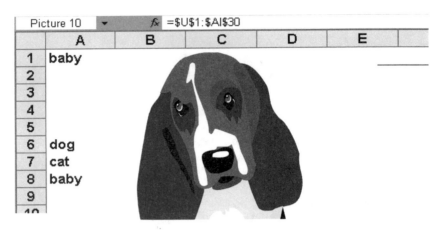

Notice the formula bar has a reference to the range originally selected when clicking the camera tool. By the way: this works *much* better with gridlines turned off, otherwise the gridlines are part of the picture. You also need to format the picture to have no border:

Select the picture, use Format/picture:

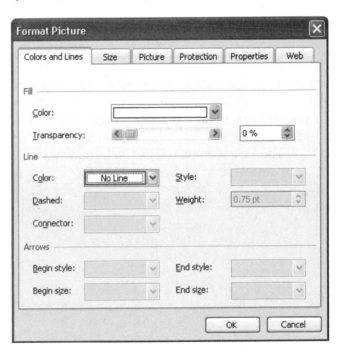

Now define Pic as =OFFSET(Sheet1!$U$1,which-1,0,30,15). The U1 is the top left cell for all the pictures; "which" we will define in a moment, the 0 means 0 columns away from column U, and the 30, 15 is the shape of the picture: 30 rows x 15 columns.

"pix" is the list of legitimate picture names—in this example, A6:A8. "which" is defined as =MATCH(Sheet1!$A$1,pix,0)*30-29. An example will help. To see the dog, we type dog in A1. The MATCH statement matches A1 against pix and that part of the formula returns 1 since dog is the first item in the range A6:A8. So, 1*30-29 is 1: (30-29). So, "which" is 1, which-1 is 0, and that makes Pic be OFFSET(U1,0,0,30,15), or the original range U1:AI30.

So where are we using pic? Remember seeing $U$1:$AI$30 once we clicked the camera tool? Select that in the formula bar and type =pic:

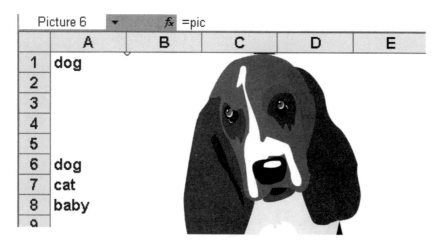

One more example and we're done. If we type *baby* in A1, then the MATCH statement matches "baby" against pix and that part returns 3 since baby is the third item in the range A6:A8. So 3*30-29 is 61: (90-29). So, "which" is 61, and which-1 is 60. That makes Pic be OFFSET(U1,60,0,30,15), or the range U61:AI90. That exactly covers the picture of the baby, so the picture switches.

This is involved, but the impact is great.

76. Pulling cells together

If you have data separated by many rows that you want to put in a contiguous range of cells (see below), this will show you how you can do it easily.

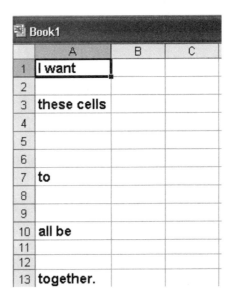

1. Select the column containing the data
2. Use Edit/Go to Special, selecting formulas or constants

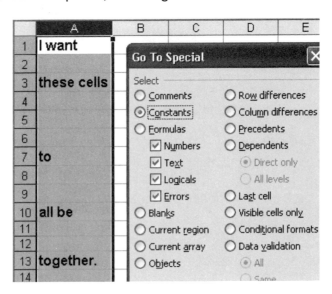

3. Copy

	A
1	I want
2	
3	these cells
4	
5	
6	
7	to
8	
9	
10	all be
11	
12	
13	together.

4. Click in new location and paste

	A	B	C
1	I want		I want
2			these cells
3	these cells		to
4			all be
5			together.
6			
7	to		
8			
9			
10	all be		
11			
12			
13	together.		

The results will always be constants, not formulas, even if they were originally formulas.

77. Protecting ranges from insertion of rows/columns

You can put an array formula to the left or on top of ranges to be protected from inadvertent insertions. Suppose you have a table of values in N33:R70 which isn't always in view, so you (or someone else) might accidentally insert a row at A44 and destroy the integrity of the table (if it were being used in a lookup formula, the blank row in it would likely create errors).

In M33:M70, a parallel 1-column range, array-enter =0 (that's hold Ctrl+Shift, when entering =0):

	M33	▼	f_x {=0}	
	L	M	N	O
32				
33		0	Protected range	Protected range	Pr
34		0	Protected range	Protected range	Pr
35		0	Protected range	Protected range	Pr
36		0	Protected range	Protected range	Pr
37		0	Protected range	Protected range	Pr
38		0	Protected range	Protected range	Pr

You'll see {=0}, indicating the range is array-entered.
If you try to insert rows you get the "you cannot change part of an array" message:

Notice that the protected range is out of sight and we're trying to insert a row at row 37 which would put a blank into that remote range.

78. Getting to your Visual Basic routine by F5 (Go to) from the worksheet

If you know the name of your Visual Basic subroutine you can get to it quickly just as if it were a range name! This assumes, of course, that the VBA project is not protected!

Edit/Go to (F5) and enter the name of the procedure! This is also true if you type the name in the Name box.

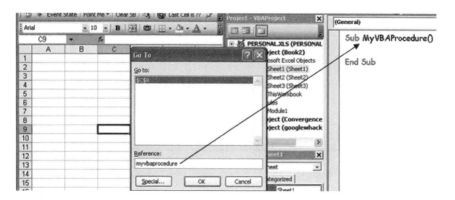

79. Getting to Workbook events

Perhaps you know that you can get to work*sheet* events by right-clicking the sheet tab and selecting "View Code". But did you know that you can get to the work*book* events just as easily? Right-click the Excel *LOGO* near the file menu and select View code—you're right at the Workbook events! If there are no events yet coded, simply pull down the left dropdown and select "Workbook". (If there *are* workbook events already coded, you're taken to them.)

80. Aligning UserForm objects

Selecting more than one object will show one with white handles, others with black handles.

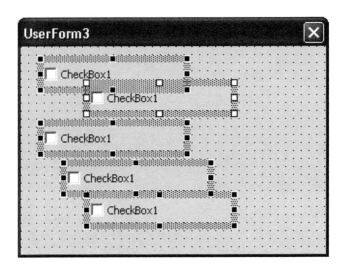

Notice the 2nd one has white handles. This one is the one used for aligning:

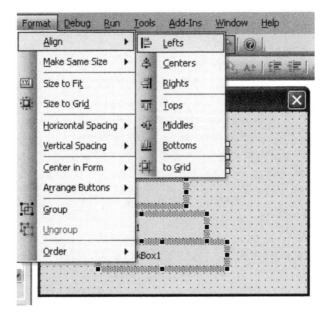

This becomes:

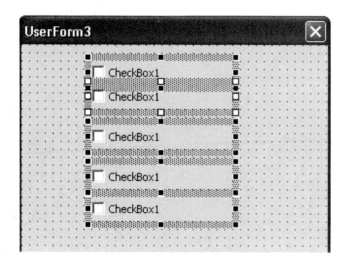

VBA

81. Put pictures in UserForms from the clipboard

Copy any picture into the clipboard.

Access the UserForm, and click in the Picture property:

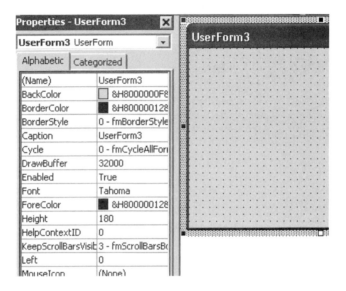

Even though the picture you want is in the clipboard, the Paste command in the Edit menu is dim. But you can paste into the picture property with Ctrl/v.

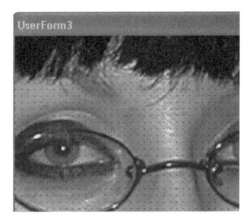

You can remove the picture via Ctrl/x.

82. *Make your own tools for forms*

You're always creating and OK and Cancel pair of buttons, right? Well, you can save them. Select them both and drag directly onto the toolbox.

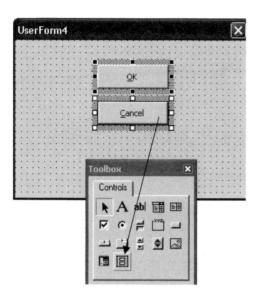

VBA

You can then use this new tool to drag both OK and Cancel buttons onto any new UserForm.

If you right-mouse click this new tool, you get

and by selecting "Customize New Group," you will see these options:

which you can edit (Edit Picture) to become:

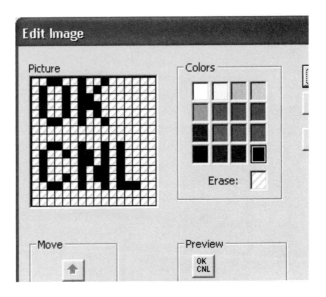

You can save *any* combinations for easy future development. And they're available in all future sessions of Excel to drag out of the toolbox onto your form. Only the design is kept, not any code behind the objects.

You can also place these on your own Controls "page"—if you right-click the Controls tab you'll see this:

Selecting New Page and right-clicking this tab, and you'll see:

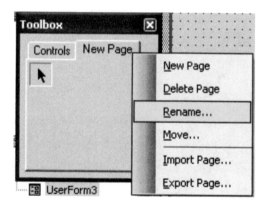

...which yields:

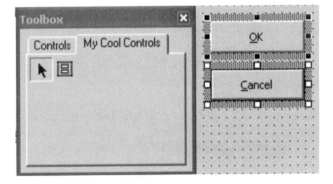

...or

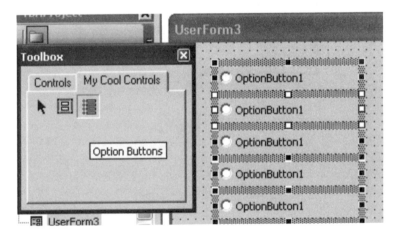

And now you can see you can store a whole *library* of controls:

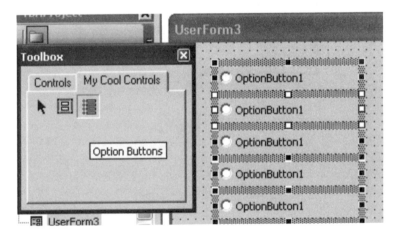

Just drag them from the control toolbox onto your UserForm!

VBA

83. *Using invisible objects*

Suppose you have this simple form:

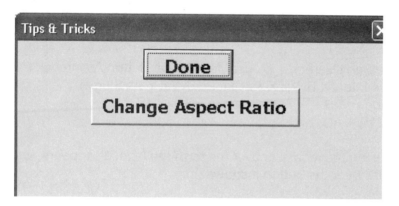

Wouldn't it be cool to show text simply by hovering (no click necessary) the mouse over an object? We'll show how you can have "Here's the explanation you wanted...blah blah blah" when the cursor moves over the "Change Aspect Ratio" button:

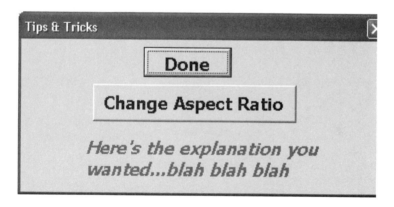

Here's the "magic" code to do that. First, the label has its "visible" property set to False, so it doesn't show up when you first show the form. Here's the code for the MouseMove event over the Done button:

```
Private Sub CommandButton2_MouseMove(ByVal Button As Integer,
ByVal Shift As Integer, ByVal X As Single, ByVal Y As Single)
Me.Label1.Visible = True
End Sub
```

The "meat" of this command is simply to make the label ("Label1") visible. So whenever the mouse hovers over the button you see it. But you also need to make the label *invisible* when the mouse is no longer hovering over the button. There's no MouseNoLongerMove event! So, you need to place another mouse move event over the form itself:

```
Private Sub UserForm_MouseMove(ByVal Button As Integer, ByVal
Shift As Integer, ByVal X As Single, ByVal Y As Single)
Me.Label1.Visible = False
End Sub
```

Now, when the mouse is over the form the label disappears, and when it's over the button it shows up.

VBA

84. Initialize Listboxes, Comboboxes with months via GetCustomListContents

Much more efficient than setting up some range containing the list of months, you can put this code into the initialize event of the form:

```
Private Sub UserForm_Initialize()
Me.ListBox1.List = Application.GetCustomListContents(4)
End Sub
```

Application.GetCustomListContents(4) refers to the 4th item in the Tools/Options/Custom List:

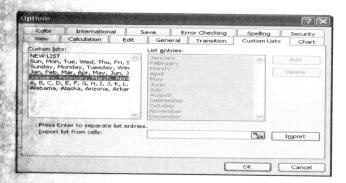

If you want to show days of the week, you'd use Application.GetCustomListContents(2)!

85. *Using Microsoft Visual Basic bookmarks*

Microsoft Visual Basic has an Edit Toolbar which has, among other things, the ability to put bookmarks into your code, temporarily (they won't save).

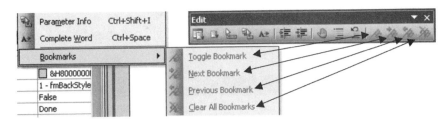

It makes getting to a location in code *very* easy to access. It shows up as a blue flag in the margin of the code:

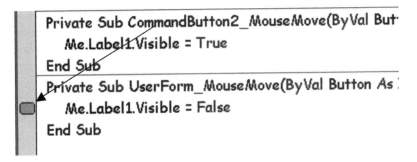

You can mark code even across projects, and as you click the Next or Previous Bookmark button, it will immediately take you to that section of code.

You can even bookmark the immediate window(!), but you won't see the indicator because the immediate window has no margin. But you'll see the cursor blinking in the immediate window.

Index

Index

Picture Credits: pp. 122, 123, 124, 126, 127 Totem Graphics; pp. 123, 124, PhotoDisc.

Index

Changing cell reference

If you have a reference such as =SUM(A500:A525) and need to change it to =SUM(A525:A535), you would most likely edit the formula and change the 500 to 525 and the 525 to 535. And of course, that would work. Did you know you can just change the 500 to 535 and get the same result? That is, you would see this before pressing enter:

but as soon as you entered the formula, you'd see:

Excel would change it for you!

A few miscellaneous Shortcuts

• Ctrl/' (single apostrophe) – this copies the cell above exactly. So, if cell A1 has =SUM($B2:C7), then pressing Ctrl/' from cell A2 will put =SUM($B2:C7) in cell A2.

• Ctrl/" (double-quote) – this copies the value from the cell above. So if cell A1 has =SUM(E1:E10) and it's value is 350, then pressing Ctrl/" from cell A2 will put the plain number 350 in cell A2.

• Ctrl/; will put in today's date

• Ctrl/: will put in the time.

• If you press Ctrl/; followed by a space then Ctrl/:, you'll have the date and the time.

• Shift/F2 will insert a Comment

• F9 will calculate the open workbooks; Shift/F9 will calculate the active workbook

Finding after the Find dialog is closed

Shift/F4 repeats find after find was done; Shift/Ctrl/F4 repeats find backwards!
That is, if you did a normal Find command to find something:

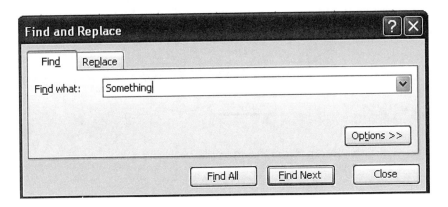

then if you close the find command and use Shift/F4, it will still find the same text, and Shift/Ctrl/F4 will find the same text backwards.